W9-BCU-646

MARRIAGE:

FIELDING'S

MIRROR

OF

MORALITY

MARRIAGE:

FIELDING'S

MIRROR

OF

MORALITY

823.
5
FIELDING

BY

MURIAL BRITTAIN WILLIAMS

Studies In The Humanities
Literature

The University of Alabama Press
University, Alabama

75-22211

For

D.L., David, and Mark

Copyright (c) 1973
By University of Alabama Press
ISBN Number 0-8173-7311-X
Library of Congress Catalog Card Number 73-56
Manufactured in the United States of America

CONTENTS

ACKNOWLEDGMENTS

I owe much to a number of friends and colleagues who have assisted and encouraged me in the preparation of this study of Fielding, but I am particularly indebted to four whose good counsel and enthusiasm have enriched my life as well as this book: Miss Elizabeth Coleman, Miss Sara Mayfield, Dr. Robert M. Wallace, and especially Dr. Samuel G. Hornsby, who has listened, read, and advised with apparently inexhaustible patience.

INTRODUCTION

Henry Fielding's literary career, 1727-1754, coincides with a period when social and economic changes were making profound alterations in the pattern of eighteenth-century life, and consequently requiring reevaluation of many long-accepted standards of morality. None caused a greater verbal outburst than the marriage question. Few writers of the age had more to say on the subject than Fielding. As a lawyer and a magistrate, Fielding was acutely aware of the legal and moral ramifications of this issue; as a writer, he reflects the issue in its purely human effects and in the contemporary setting.

The marriage debate resolved itself around two fundamental concepts of morality: Should marriage be based on romantic love or on prudential considerations; should the parent or the child have the right of picking the marriage partner. These questions are actually outward expressions of more fundamental forces at work—the emergence of the middle class and the changing status of women. An increasingly significant middle class was beginning to center its worldly aspirations around successful marriage and simultaneously to insist upon a morality endowing such an advantageous match with the sanction of romance as well. A "successful" marriage was one which increased the fortunes and raised the social status. The position of women, especially of the middle class, was changing drastically because of a decline of industry in the home and the corresponding mechanization and centralization of industry. Many women, who had formerly contributed to the income of the family by such tasks as weaving in the home, were no longer productive and were therefore less essential to the home

1

economy. Thus, women were insisting upon and gaining,
though gradually, greater independence in choosing their marriage partners—indeed even choosing not to marry—at a time
when paradoxically they were more dependent than ever upon
the necessity of making their way by a favorable marriage.

Controversies over marriage and women's status are,
obviously, not an issue new to the literature of the eighteenth
century, as witness the mass of material on the subject in The
Canterbury Tales, but the degree and kind are distinctive.
The medieval interest in this subject, reflected by Chaucer,
revolved around the theological disputes—the superiority of the
celibate over the married state and the supposed moral inferiority of woman—rather than the social and personal aspects which engaged the eighteenth century. The eighteenth
century was the culminating moment in the process of cultural
change when the break with the inheritance of the past was
perceptible to all, however varied the reactions.

Before the emergence of the novel, the comic drama was
the literary form which traditionally used domestic life as the
subject of much of its stock humor. With a bit of change in the
window dressing, the situations and dialogue of classical comedy could pass for Restoration comedy, with marriage as the
stock-in-trade butt of satire. Marriage as a subject for jest
is obviously not limited to any particular period, but in no
age before the Restoration had attitudes toward marriage been
so contemptuous and flippant, nor marriage so much a preoccupation of the drama. G.S. Alleman catalogs the dramatic
commonplaces of Restoration comedy thus:[1]

> Young gallants pretend aversion to marriage only to re-
> pent and accept it in the fifth act. Parents plan unions
> involving money, land and social position only to be frus-
> trated by children who defy them by marrying for love.
> Covetous old men, town fops, and ridiculous country
> knights plan to marry wealth and beauty only to find
> themselves linked to chambermaids—or worse.

Although the hey-day of the Restoration comedy was over by

1700, many Restoration attitudes, themselves survivals of a long tradition, continued into the eighteenth century. (See Appendix.) One of the strongest of these was an attitude of cynical contempt for love and marriage, which the Spectator (No. 525, Nov. 1, 1712) complains provide "a standing jest in all clubs of mirth and gay conversation." Not only was infidelity winked at, but fidelity was mocked; a "state of wedlock was the common mark of all the adventurers in a farce or comedy."

The closing years of the seventeenth century and the first quarter of the eighteenth century witnessed a strong and very vocal reaction against such frivolous disregard for the sanctity of marriage and seeming approval of outright licentiousness. The protest is usually attributed to the increasing influence of middle-class standards of morality, but it must at least in some measure have been an inevitable reaction, unrestricted as to class, against characters who lacked many of the normal emotions of ordinary men. The corrective impulse resulted in a sudden eruption of sentimental comedies filled with nauseously exemplary characters and overtly instructive content.

It was not to be the sentimental comedy, however, which gave true voice to the attitudes of the century concerning love and marriage; perhaps because the mingling of laughter and tears created, as Oliver Goldsmith insisted, a bastard type which violated truth to human nature, perhaps because no really great playwright appeared to meld the types. Whatever the cause, from the moment of Pamela's arrival on the scene in 1740, the novel served as the literary outlet for the marriage debate. In fact, it is not too sweeping a statement to say that this new form evolved primarily to accommodate the new ideas concerning the aspirations of the middle class and specifically new attitudes toward marriage.

Henry Fielding began his career in this literary environment of changing intellectual currents. No other single author of the century provides so rich and so comprehensive a body of material for examining this issue. As an author, he came to the novel after an apprenticeship in the drama in imitation of Restoration plays; his interest can be traced from his

earliest efforts as a writer of comedies (1727-1737) through
the flowering of his art in the novels (1741-1751).

In his earliest treatment of the subject of marriage, Fielding unquestionably reflects Restoration models in form, subject, and tone, more than personal conviction. He himself
declared that, as a novice, he chose a career as hackney
writer in preference to hackney coachman. Though the remark
was probably facetious, obviously the type best proven for immediate financial returns was the Restoration comedy. In
choosing this type, even if only for the hope of remuneration,
he was joining ranks with the realists and satirists. Following
the end of his theatrical career with the passage of the Licensing Act of 1737, he moved steadily in the direction of moralistic purpose, which had been evident from the first dramatic
efforts designed to laugh men out of their follies and vices.
His final achievement as a novelist was a pioneering effort in
the serious study of problems after marriage. In the novels
Fielding reacted consciously and sharply to what he considered
false morality concerning marriage, sparked by the success
of Pamela.

The essential character of Fielding's social and moral outlook is revealed in his attitude toward marriage: in the social
circumstances, the personal traits, the ethical and economic
considerations requisite in his judgment for that happiness in
marriage which he described as the highest felicity of which
men are capable in this life. This moral outlook can be best
understood in the framework of the times and in the light of
certain restrictions inherent in the satiric mode that Fielding
chose for presenting his views.

It has long been recognized that Fielding, by birth linked
with the upper class, is essentially conservative in his concept
of a stratified social structure, concerned less than some of
his contemporaries with social mobility—the interpenetration
and realignment of emergent groups. Events, particularly in
the novels, work themselves out in the direction of preserving
the division of classes in accord with the established social
situation. Specifically, his heroes, whatever their personal
status and class may seem to be, arrive at a proper gentility

and financial competence by the end of the novel: the servant Joseph and the illegitimate Tom find satisfactorily genteel fathers; Billy Booth, through his wife's recovered inheritance, achieves financial security. Fielding saw a stratified society as the most desirable pattern, and he accepted rather complacently certain conditions implied in that order. By implication, for example, marriage within one's own class is generally the pattern, though not the first requisite, for successful marriage. His writing, at least up to Amelia, displays a confidence in the possibility of solving the problems of his world within the established framework. It was not necessary to remake the social system but rather to rectify the errors of individual human beings.

An essential part of Fielding's confidence in this order was the need, even the duty, to question the values and the conduct of the individuals in society. He faces the basic questions involved in the marriage debate by resorting to the classic conflict between parent and child over marriage. The parent, predictably, desires a marriage economically and socially advantageous; the child refuses on the grounds of personal preference for another temporarily unsuitable but more attractive choice: thus Sophia's preference for Tom over Blifil. The pattern is the same in the choice of the hero, as Booth's preference for Amelia over Miss Matthews. Fielding, however, never makes the choice one of romantic considerations alone. The chosen mate is characteristically morally superior, and on the issue of morality Fielding constructs his tales. The solving of external difficulties hinges upon the hero's arrival at a state of moral maturity. The lessons to be learned in the hero's educative process give Fielding the frame for the social ills he wishes to depict. Moreover, Fielding tests the morality of his characters in the broadest sense of the word. The ordeal of Billy Booth and the education of Tom Jones, no less than the journey of Joseph Andrews and Parson Adams, are pilgrimages of challenge to the standards acceptable to powerful segments of society but not to right-minded men, whether the challenge involves chastity or charity or privilege. It is almost impossible to separate Fielding's social ideas from his

concepts of morality, in marriage as in other areas; for the
injustices which he attacked have their beginning in violation
of morality and their result in social evils.

By such a challenging of morality in its broadest terms,
Fielding confronts us with numerous situations which require
the evaluation of various kinds of violations of morality and
convention. It is immoral for a parent to force a marriage on
an unwilling child, though the practice has social sanction
based on nominal service to the Biblical injunction of filial
obedience; for Fielding, it is right for the child to defy such a
convention based on disregard for human dignity. It does not
follow that Fielding sanctions defiance of parents. In fact,
even in a case where the disobedience is justified, he shows
the consequences as inevitably painful. There is a higher
morality than social convention and a higher satisfaction than
conformity that should lie at the heart of all human conduct; it
is this which concerns Fielding and shapes the portraits of
marriage which he gives. The foundation of morality is humane feeling and right reason on a purely secular plane; and
charity, on the Christian.

The moral sense is necessary to a happy marriage, as it is
necessary to a happy life. The most significant of all human
relations, if it is to be successful, argues Fielding, must be
founded on love; but it is a love akin to the charity which the
New Testament admonishes all men to practice toward their
fellow men. Benevolence, which Fielding equated with Christian charity, seemed to him a necessary basis of the selfless
love requisite for marriage. Fielding's detestation of the com-
mercialization of marriage, the degrading of the human relationship for material motives, stemmed from this basic morality rather than from a disregard for the practical necessities of the married state. Marriage, as practiced for mercenary gain, he saw as a game in which two people cheated
each other of everything they could. He emphasized his heroines' right principles in marrying on the basis of the merit of
the partner, not his social status. A corresponding emphasis
was placed on the heroines' superiority of mind and character
rather than physical beauty as the source of their greatest at-

traction. The goodness of the object is the ultimate source of happiness in love. Squire Allworthy enumerates the bases of marriage as love, religion, virtue, and sense. These, love being interpreted in its Biblical connotations, are also ideally the bases for all human relations.

It is customary, then, to label Fielding as a conservative in his concept of social order, but any harmony within that order depended upon the goodness of the human beings who made up the classes. One may agree that his was largely a conservative outlook if judged by proposals for changes in the institutions of society, but he is a radical of the most profound sort if judged by his espousal of the true Christian ideal. When the ethics of that ideal are practiced, Fielding would have maintained, the revolution in men's inner lives will eliminate the need for changes in institutions.

Fielding chose to present these essential views in the mode of satire. In the work of every satirist there is a constant tension between the real and the ideal; the dichotomy is inherent in the satiric mode. The satirist draws his material from the disparity between the two. Just as the satirist's forte is his vitality in handling the materials of the real world, the center of criticism of any satirist is likely to be the conclusions which he draws. He presents his case against the follies and vices of society, but finally he must offer, explicitly or implicitly, an alternative, or abandon his case. The alternative is a utopia; but, paradoxically, the satirist may only lead his hero to the gates of that ideal world. He cannot enter; all utopias are unsatisfactory. Or he may return his hero to the real world, wiser in the ways of the world but unable to change that world. The latter way is the usual. Cervantes brings Quixote back to reality—and death. The best that Voltaire can do is to return Candide to cultivate his garden; Swift abandons Gulliver to the painful readaptation to his own kind after a stay with the Houyhnhnms. The controversial falling off of Huckleberry Finn after Huck's return to civilization has engaged most of Clemens' critics in the twentieth century. Fielding chooses the other route for his conclusions: all of his stories end with a kind of Eden-vision of ideal happiness-ever-after with the major problems solved, or removed; good has triumphed and evil has been chastised. This state is achieved, it should be added, only after the moral growth of the central figure. Nonetheless critical reaction has been as controversial in the case of Fielding's solutions as with the other satirists'. The happy endings are inevitable to the comic mode which Fielding chose and likewise inevitable if he is to achieve any alternative to the folly and vice portrayed. Fielding, moreover, stands more closely allied to Cervantes, his acknowledged master, than to other major satirists in that he did not move into total pessimism. Satire carries with it the seed of destruction of the satirist's own equilibrium, and the story of a satirist's career is likely to be one of progressive pessimism, ending in indignation and, occasionally, incoherence. Fielding's work darkens; but not even in <u>Amelia</u>, the most somber of his writing, does he abandon the optimism which declares itself for the possibility of a better world.

What we see in a study of Fielding's attitude toward marriage is a maturing and sobering, not a shifting, moral outlook. In every period of his career, whatever problem he attacked, he dealt with it in terms of moral rightness, whether his method was burlesque, parody, high comedy, or serious preachment.

Chapter 1

FIELDING'S MARRIAGES

Before turning to a close examination of Henry Fielding's treatment of the subject of marriage in the plays and novels, it would be well to consider those facets of his own life which no doubt shaped his view of marriage. Primary sources from which to build the story of his marriages are scanty—no letters to either his first or second wife; a single journal; only a few autobiographical comments in his fiction. The great pitfall in evaluating the material which does exist is the temptation to link Fielding too literally with the fictional lives of his creations, to assume that the youthful Fielding is Tom Jones or that Fielding after marriage is Captain Booth. Some sentiments and some events are inevitably colored by his actual experiences; occasionally he states that such is the case. It is perilous to play the game of probability, reconstructing a life for Fielding out of the adventures of his heroes. There does emerge, nonetheless, from his own scattered comments and from a variety of secondary sources, a picture of Fielding as suitor and husband that is flamboyant enough for the reader of romances and at the same time combines those elements of idealism and realism that mark all his fiction.

As a boy, Fielding experienced some squabbles over financial matters growing out of marriage settlements and division of loyalties in his own family circle. His parents, Edmund Fielding and Sarah Gould, married without the consent of Sarah's parents. There seems to have been no discord between the young husband and his in-laws until he remarried after Sarah's death. Then his mother-in-law, Lady Gould, charged Edmund with failing to use the estate left by Mrs. Fielding's

9

father for her benefit and, in the event of her death, for the proper care and education of her young children, of whom Henry was the oldest. There was protracted and bitter legal action between Lady Gould and Edmund Fielding, with charges of neglect and countercharges of malice. Finally the grandmother was given control over Sarah's children. Fielding apparently preferred living with Lady Gould, for he spent his holidays from Eton with her during the period when the case was in the process of being tried. He was not, however, alienated from his good-natured but improvident father, for he never expressed any bitterness toward him and had a deep and abiding affection for at least one of his half-brothers, John.

The earliest known romantic escapade involving Fielding reads like a chapter from any eighteenth-century abduction plot, but with comic overtones. The principals were the nineteen-year-old Fielding, at the time a handsome youth of over six feet, vigorous and manly, with a high forehead and a nose "a little inclined to the Roman"; a Miss Sarah Andrew of Lyme Regis, a beautiful fifteen-year-old orphan, heiress to a considerable estate; and two guardian-uncles, both eager to marry the young lady to an eligible son. Of Fielding's siege of Miss Andrew's heart, no written record exists. From the legal action which followed, one may surmise that the uncle with whom Sarah lived, Andrew Tucker, opposed the attentions of Fielding. Fielding persisted. The opposition increased. An attempted abduction was the next logical step, logical at least to a dashing and romantic boy, for it was an action endorsed by popular literature and not uncommon in real life.

On a Sunday, Fielding and his servant, Joseph Lewis, intercepted the carriage bearing Miss Andrew and Tucker and attempted to take Miss Andrew by force. Tucker and his men beat off the abductors, but in the exchange Tucker was beaten and bruised sufficiently to warrant his entering a complaint[2] before the mayor of the town. He swore that he was "in fear of his life or of some bodily hurt to be done to him or to be procured to be done to him by Henry Ffielding, gent, and his servant or companion." Further, he declared a special fear that Joseph Lewis would "beat, wound, maim, or kill him."

Fielding did not appear in court to answer the charge but, according to a story popular in Lyme Regis, stuck up on a wall in his own handwriting this declaration of his own:

> "Nov. 15th 1725
> This is to give notice to the world that Andrew Tucker and his son John Tucker are clowns, and cowards.
> > Witness my hand
> > Henry Ffielding"[3]

No more came of the affair as far as Fielding was concerned, but to conclude this chapter of life-in-imitation-of-literature, Mr. Tucker immediately removed Sarah for safe keeping to her other guardian, Ambrose Rhodes, who within the next year married her to his own son.

Fielding's reaction to the disappointment of losing Sarah was no more serious than to prompt a translation into burlesque verse of part of Juvenal's Sixth Satire on the shortcomings of women, sketched out, he says, before he was twenty, "all the Revenge taken by an injured lover" (Author's Preface, The Miscellanies). Within a season or so the injured lover was addressing conventional poetic tributes to a "Rosalinda" and a "Euthalia." The identity of these young ladies, if they existed at all, has never been established.

By 1728, at the age of twenty-one, Fielding was in London preparing for the performance of his first comedy, Love in Several Masques. It is tempting to link his own experience, as his biographer Cross does,[4] with that of Merital, a worthy but penniless suitor, and Helena, a beautiful heiress, whose marriage is prevented by Helena's avaricious guardian, Sir Positive Trap. It is unlikely, however, that the scars from the boyish escapade were so deep and lasting as to survive for three years. More significantly, Fielding's play in no way departs from the conventions of an almost endless number of comedies based on the arranged-marriage plot, using exactly the same circumstances and the same pattern of dialogue common to all of them.

After his first attempt as a dramatist, Fielding studied for almost two years in Leyden and then returned, now twenty-

three years old, to London, to enter the theatrical arena to
seek fame and fortune. During the rough and tumble years of
what amounted to theatrical warfare, with Fielding often at the
center, the happiest episode of his personal life occurred. By
1730 Fielding had become acquainted with the beautiful Cradock
sisters of Salisbury, Charlotte and Catherine, perhaps during
visits with his grandmother, Lady Gould, who lived not far
from the residence of the Craddocks. The praises of the girls
reached even as far as London, when a poem addressed to
them by a local poet appeared in <u>The London Magazine</u>.

At first the young playwright, who was already causing
some stir in London theatrical circles, came calling on both
sisters, but he soon chose Charlotte as the special object of
his love. In the style of the fashionable young gallant, Fielding himself turned poet to celebrate the lady's beauty and to
extol her virtue. The poems, he says, are "productions of the
heart rather than the head."

In "An Epigram" he tells the story of Jove's ecstasy with
Alcmena, for whose love Jove "kept the sun a-bed all day."
But the lover insists that were he possessed of Celia's charms
and had he Jove's power, the sun would never rise again. In
"The Question" the lover is inarticulate before Celia's demand,
"How well do you love your Celia?" Then she, pitying his distress, forgives his inability to express his love in words, for
she shares his pain. In "To Celia" the lover utters his scorn
of the pleasures of the town and all its ways, which he enumerates in twenty-nine lines, and concludes

> Ask you then, Celia, if there be
> The thing I love? my charmer, thee.
> Thee more than light, than life adores,
> Thou dearest, sweetest creature more
> Than wildest raptures can express...
>
> Let not my hatred of mankind
> Wonder within my Celia move,
> Since she possesses all my love.

"Advice to the Nymphs of New S[aru]m," the only poem of the group specifically dated (1730), tells the other beauties of the town to cease their competition with the "second Queen of Love," for it is a hopeless quest. The most original of the love poems, "Cupid Called to Account" was prompted, says Fielding in a headnote, by Celia's "apprehending her house would be broke open, and having an old fellow to guard it, who sat up all night, with a gun without any ammunition." Venus calls Cupid before her throne to answer the charge of neglect of Venus' own darling maid. Cupid answers:

"Mama, it was no fault of mine.
I in a dimple lay perdue,
That little guard-room chose by you.
A hundred Loves (all arm'd) did grace
The beauties of her neck and face;
Thence, by a sigh I dispossessed,
Was blown to Harry Fielding's breast;
Where I was forc'ed all night to stay,
Because I could not find my way.
But did mama know there what work
I've made, how acted like a Turk;
What pains, what torment he endures,
Which no physician ever cures,
She would forgive." The goddess smil'd,
And gently chuck'd her wicked child,
Bid him go back, and take more care,
And give her service to the fair.

On Celia's wishing to have a Lilliputian to play with, the lover declares he would happily be "five foot shorter" than he is to grant her whim. He fancies the delights he would enjoy being held in her hand, hiding in the plaitings of her gown, or sitting astride her hat; then night would find him keeping guard upon her pillow and surveying her beauty—a sight, alas, which would make him wish to be himself again. In an untitled poem, Venus is about to relegate rule of the earth to her fairest as

vice-regent. All the nymphs are called to put forward their
claims. Suddenly Jove interrupts the proceedings and thunders
his judgment:

> And can you, daughter, doubt to whom
> (He cried) belongs the happy doom,
> While C—cks yet make bless'd the earth
> C—cks, who long before their birth,
> I, by your own petition mov'd,
> Decreed to be by all belov'd.
> C—cks, to whose celestial dower
> I gave all beauties in my power;
> To form whose lovely minds and faces,
> I stripp'd half heaven of its graces.
> Oh let them bear an equal sway,
> So shall mankind well-pleas'd obey."
> The god thus spoke, the goddess bow'd...
> And Cupid glad writ down their name.

All the poems have a sprightly wit and charm, but they are
conventional tributes, such as might be addressed to any young
woman of beauty and good disposition by any suitor with a
knack for versifying and a saving dash of humor. The really
memorable descriptions of Charlotte were written long after
her death, in the fictional guise of Sophia in Tom Jones and the
heroine in Amelia. Though they are colored by the fact that
they are memorials, "of one whose imagine never can depart
from [his] breast," they are vivid and detailed enough to leave
little doubt of the reality of Charlotte's beauty of person and
character.

> Sophia [or Charlotte] was a middle-sized woman, but
> rather inclining to tall. Her shape was not only exact,
> but extremely delicate; and the nice proportion of her
> arms promised the truest symmetry in her limbs. Her
> hair, which was black, was so luxuriant, that it reached
> her middle, before she cut it to comply with the modern
> fashion; and it was now curled so gracefully in her neck,

that few could believe it to be her own. If envy could find any part of the face which demanded less commendation than the rest, it might possibly think her forehead might have been higher without prejudice to her. Her eyebrows were full, even, and arched beyond the power of art to imitate. Her black eyes had a lustre in them, which all her softness could not extinguish. Her nose was exactly regular, and her mouth, in which were two rows of ivory, exactly answered Sir John Suckling's description in those lines:—

Her lips were red, and one was thin,
Compared to that was next her chin,
Some bee had stung it newly.

Her cheeks were of the oval kind; and in her right she had a dimple, which the least smile discovered. Her chin had certain its share in forming the beauty of her face.... Her complexion had more of the lily than of the rose.... Her neck was long and finely turned; and here if I was not afraid of offending her delicacy, I might justly say, the highest beauties of the famous Venus de Medicis were outdone. Here was whiteness which no lilies, ivory, nor alabaster could match.

So much for the exquisite physical beauty of Fielding's Sophia-Charlotte. Her beauty of mind was "every way equal to her person.... When she smiled the sweetness of her temper diffused that glory over her countenance of which no regularity of features can give." She was perfectly well-bred, with a reticence and modesty which are the chief qualities praised in Sophia by Squire Allworthy.

The picture is repeated in Amelia, with somewhat less attention to physical beauty and more to the sweetness of temper and beauty of character. In fact, Booth insists that his first feeling for Amelia was based on admiration of her character rather than infatuation with her beauty, which drew many suitors. Amelia is in its entirety a testament to the qualities which Fielding idealized in woman, and his own testimony is that he knew them in Charlotte.

A four-year courtship ended with marriage on November 28, 1734. Even in the matter of the wedding ceremony there is just the dash of mystery that intrigues biographers. The marriage was solemnized in St. Mary's Church at Charl-combe, a parish nearly two miles north of Bath, with Fielding and Charlotte listed as being of the Parish of St. James, in Bath, rather than of their own parish in Salisbury. Cross speculates that the actual marriage was a "sudden impulse af-ter a protracted courtship" or even an elopement such as that rendered in Amelia to escape a mother's objection. He contin-ues that perhaps the new son-in-law was soon accepted, as was Booth by Amelia's mother, and so on.[5] There is not a shred of real evidence for these surmises; the most prosaic reasons may have lain behind the unceremonious occasion of a quiet wedding in a small nearby chapel. The plot of Amelia, chil-dren marrying in opposition to a parent's will, had already been the material of several plays by Fielding as well as the material of so many standard romances as to be uncountable. The fact of the matter, and the only fact known, is that the two were married and shortly afterward settled in London, where Fielding continued his efforts as a dramatist.

Further evidence that Fielding did not extend his own ex-perience directly into his plays at least is the fact that his first comedies after marriage are An Old Man Taught Wisdom, in which one character was hissed so thoroughly for his dis-paraging remarks about women that Fielding eliminated him before the second performance; and The Universal Gallant, which even Cross acknowledges contained the most caustic remarks on the frailties of women penned up to this time by Fielding[6]—these within three months after the marriage which gave him the greatest happiness he knew, to a wife he called "the most excellent of women."

The most excellent of women was to share trials enough with her husband in the ten years of marriage that ensued. Fielding's success varied from play to play. When money was in hand, Fielding spent it lavishly. At the best moments of his last two years in the theatre, such as the 60-odd nights of Pasquin's run, his success was so great as to be noted in a

contemporary cartoon showing the Queen of Common Sense
pouring gold into his lap. But his success was short-lived.
1736 was marked personally by the birth of the first child, a
daughter named for her mother, and professionally by Fielding's deeper involvement in the turmoil of politics. So effective was he that his contemporaries considered him to be the
chief target of Walpole's Licensing Act, which was passed in
June of 1737, closing the theatres to Fielding. The young family returned to East Stour to plan a new venture.

With the theatres closed to him and no immediate prospects
in literature and the family situation made more critical by
the birth of a second daughter in 1737, Fielding turned to the
study of law. An inheritance from Charlotte's mother and
Fielding's share in the estate of his mother tided the family
over the period of transition. The records of the family's living arrangements are confused during this period. The best
guess is that for at least one year Fielding lived near the Middle Temple and left the family in Salisbury. Apparently he
rented quarters near the Temple for the whole family in 1740.

In late 1739 Fielding had begun his first newspaper, The
Champion. He was once more vigorously involved in contemporary events, facing with great gusto many of his old adver-
saries. Of domestic affairs there is no mention. One can assume it was a satisfying period for both husband and wife, even
if difficult financially, with Charlotte caring for her family and
Fielding studying law and participating in the whirl of political
events, a life he found engrossing. In the midst of his study of
law and journalistic work, he was about to enter still a third,
and the most momentous, phase of his career. His personal
life was also about to take a turn for the worse.

His own Champion carried in its November 6, 1740, issue
an announcement of the publication of Pamela: or Virtue Rewarded. The rest of that story is part of the legend of literature. On April 4, 1741, appeared An Apology for the Life of
Shamela Andrews and Fielding's career as a novelist was
launched. In February, 1742, Joseph Andrews was published.

What can be ascertained of the year of the composition of
Joseph Andrews suggests that the bright world of Joseph and

his friend Abraham Adams was created out of a period of agony
for the Fieldings. During the winter Fielding had suffered a
severe attack of gout, which was to plague him the rest of his
life. He says that at the same time "a favorite child," his
first daughter Charlotte, was dying in one bed and his wife was
desperately ill in another. Little Charlotte did indeed die and
was buried just a few weeks after the publication of Joseph Andrews. In the year that followed, Fielding's output is prolific
and undistinguished; there is a note of desperation in the quantity of his efforts. He gathered what he considered the best of
this and other unpublished work into The Miscellanies (1743),
probably hoping to benefit from the stir caused by the earlier
novels. The only work of permanent interest in the collection
is Jonathan Wild.

The personal situation of the family worsened. Charlotte
never fully recovered from her own illness and grief over the
loss of her first child. In 1744 Fielding took Charlotte to Bath
in the hope that the waters would do some good. She did not
rally. According to tradition passed on by Fielding's first
biographer and recorded in Lady Bute's memoirs, she caught
a fever and died in the arms of her husband. She was buried
on November 14, 1744, beside her daughter at St. Martin's in
the Fields.

Fielding's grief was such that his friends feared for a time
that he would lose his reason. Thus ended the love affair and
marriage which Fielding could never erase from his memory.

Fielding's second marriage is less picturesquely ideal. It
took place on November 27, 1747, almost exactly three years
after the death of Charlotte. The second wife was Mary Daniel, Charlotte's maid who had stayed on as housekeeper for
Fielding and his young daughter Harriet. Mary was twenty-six,
by report a good but very ugly woman. Fielding was forty, his
health already broken. It is not difficult to imagine the jests
and abuse leveled at Fielding, who had provided his enemies
an irresistible opportunity of scoffing not only at his choice of
a "cook-wench" for a wife but also at the immediate reason
for the marriage. A son was born four months after the ceremony. Indeed, some of his enemies were vicious in their

malice. Horace Walpole, revenging old grudges on his father's behalf, records an incident of two friends calling on Fielding and finding him in the company of a blind man and a whore. The blind man was his brother John, later Justice Fielding, and the "whore" was Mary Daniel Fielding. The most ironically humorous comment came from Richardson who, apparently unconscious of the irony, condemned Fielding for low conduct, for in fact living Richardson's own plot in <u>Pamela</u>.

Reviled though Mary Fielding was for lack of beauty and low station, the marriage was a satisfactory one. Lady Louisa Stuart, granddaughter of Fielding's cousin Lady Mary Wortley Montagu, recalls in her memoirs the story of the marriage told by Lady Mary:

> ... after the death of this charming woman [Charlotte] he married her maid. And yet the act was not so discreditable to his character as it may sound. The maid had few personal charms, but was an excellent creature, devotedly attached to her mistress, and almost brokenhearted for her loss. In the first agonies of his own grief, which approached to frenzy, he found no relief but from weeping with her; nor solace, when a degree calmer, but in talking to her of the angel they mutually regretted. This made her his habitual confidential associate, and in process of time he began to think he could not give his children a tenderer mother, or secure for himself a more faithful housekeeper and nurse. At least this was what he told his friends; and it is certain that her conduct as his wife confirmed it, and fully justified his good opinion.[7]

This description obviously omits the immediate urgency of Mary Daniel's pregnancy as one of the considerations.

In support of the account, Fielding has himself left an eloquent testimonial to the loyalty and devotion of Mary in <u>The Journal of a Voyage to Lisbon</u>, the record of a futile trip made in the hope of improving his health. It was necessary for the Fieldings to leave their four young children, all under seven years of age, in the care of a nurse. Only Charlotte's daughter, Harriet, accompanied them. Fielding reveals his own deep love of his family in the description of the farewells.

Wednesday, June 26, 1754
... By the light of this sun I was, in my own opinion, last to behold and take leave of some of those creatures on whom I doted with a mother-like fondness, guided by nature and passion, and uncured and unhardened by all the doctrines of that philosophical school where I had learned to bear pains and to despise death.
In this situation, as I could not conquer Nature, I submitted entirely to her, and she made as great a fool of me as she had ever done of any woman whatsoever; under pretence of giving me leave to enjoy, she drew me in to suffer, the company of my little ones during eight hours [the time of sailing had been deferred]; and I doubt not whether, in that time, I did not undergo more than in all my distemper.

Mary, who endured agonies on the voyage both physical (a severe toothache and seasickness) and mental (separation from her children), was described by Fielding as more of a heroine and philosopher than himself. His gallantry toward her until the end of his life is appealingly testified to by an incident which occurred aboard ship just before sailing. The two were sitting in their cabin when they were visited by

two ruffians, whose appearance greatly corresponded with that of the sheriffs, or rather the knight-marshal's bailiffs. One of these especially, who seemed to affect a more than ordinary degree of rudeness and insolence, came in without any kind of ceremony, with a broad gold lace on his hat, which was cocked with much military fierceness on his head. An inkhorn at his button-hole and some papers in his hand sufficiently assured me what he was, and I asked him if he and his companion were not custom-house officers: he answered... that

they were, as an information which he seemed to conclude would strike the hearer with awe... but, on the contrary, I proceeded to ask of what rank he was in the custom-house, and receiving an answer from his companion... that the gentleman was a riding surveyor, I replied
that he might be a riding surveyor, but could be no gentleman, for that none who had any title to that denomi-
nation would break into the presence of a lady without an
apology or even moving his hat. He then took his cover-
ing from his head and laid it on the table, saying, he
asked pardon....

The journey for his health, advised by his physician in Au-
gust, 1753, with great urgency, was delayed in order for
Fielding to carry out pressing and demanding magisterial work
to apprehend a gang of street robbers who were plaguing the
city of London. The effort took almost a year and the success
he had was, as he knew, probably at the cost of his life. But
he says that he despaired of that anyway and sacrificed himself
not so much in the name of patriotism as love for his family.
It was his hope that the gratitude of the public for his services
would express itself in provision for his family.

Fielding's great concern for his family is evident not only
in his own labors in their behalf but also in the earnest solici-
tation to his brother John to care for them. On Fielding's
death in October of 1754, John assumed and fulfilled the responsibility for his brother's family. Mary outlived Fielding
forty-eight years and died at the age of eighty-two, in 1802.

Fielding appears from the record to have been a man characterized by real gallantry toward women; his marriage to
Mary no less than his idealized love for Charlotte is proof of
the fact in an age when his contemporaries ridiculed him not
for the reason for the marriage but only for his wife's low station. He was a man capable of great tenderness and family affection and one who inspired devotion, tenderness, and loyalty
in return. Whether either ever spoke Amelia's declaration:
"You have a wife who will think herself happy with you, and
endeavor to make you so, in any situation," both Charlotte and

Mary lived such loyalty and devotion.

To say that Fielding's idealization of women and marriage grow out of his own experience is of course partly true. His idealism is evident, however, from the beginning of his career to the end, before marriage and after. Modeled Sophia and Amelia may be on Charlotte; but, more realistically, she too is the embodiment of an ideal which existed in Fielding's mind before the ideal took on human or fictional form.

Chapter 2

MARRIAGE IN THE PLAYS

Henry Fielding's comedies sum up the attitudes toward marriage inherited from the medieval tradition as transmitted through the Restoration comedy of the immediately preceding era and also contain the first expression of the attitudes which characterize Fielding's later, mature views. The twenty-five or so plays[8] are a catalog of the contemporary hodge-podge of types into which the eighteenth-century comedy was deteriorating: manners, burlesque, rehearsal, farce, ballad-opera, political satire, and sentimental comedy. A single play frequently combines several types, for example, The Grub Street Opera, a burlesque, a political satire, and a ballad-opera. In fact, it is a rare play of Fielding's that is limited to one genre. Whatever the type, all share the satirical intent which was the consistent aim in Fielding's art, and thus take their place in the moral scheme of his work as a whole.

Two "schools" predominate in the comedy of the era, the older Restoration tradition of the satirical comedy of manners which "aimed at humorously reflecting and criticizing the actual social scene... [accepting] the moral code actually operative in their day and... content to permit it to express itself in their plays," and the new moralized sentimental comedy which demanded that the code of human conduct expressed in comedy should be better than that in effect in life, and that comedy should recommend these higher ideals by presenting characters who exemplify them and by punishing their opposites.[9]

Although Fielding did not entirely escape the influence of the new comedy, he joined ranks with the satirists in the Restoration tradition. Like his predecessors, Fielding used love,

courtship, and marriage as the material for his comic and
satiric purpose. There are two basic patterns in the Restoration love-game comedy, however infinitely the details may be
varied. These plots are so completely formalized as to require
no detailed analysis, play by play. One pairs off a varying
number of couples, usually of different rank and age. The
complication is initiated and sustained by the conflict between
avaricious guardians and children over an arranged marriage
based on financial considerations, with interest centered around
the lovers' ingenuity in thwarting their guardians. The second
plot concerns the love intrigues of couples already married;
the interest lies in the various stratagems of wives and their
lovers to cuckold husbands and of husbands to rule and restrain
their wives. There is no sympathy for the husband; it is a
cardinal principle of Restoration comedy that cuckolds make
themselves. Obviously the two plot patterns can be easily
combined and usually are, though one theme predominates.

Fielding's pertinent plays* for the most part follow these
two plot-types closely. His farces, by their very nature, present the most exaggerated portrayal of marriage and show lit-

---

*
The following plays, on the basis of the main plot line, offer
the best commentary on the subject of marriage. Arranged-
marriage plot: An Old Man Taught Wisdom (1735); Love in
Several Masques (1728); The Temple Beau, (1730); The Fathers (n. d.); The Miser (1732); The Wedding Day (n. d.);
Marital-infidelity plot: The Letter Writers (1731); The Modern Husband (1732); The Universal Gallant (1735). Many of the
other plays use the arranged-marriage plot as a secondary
motif, for example, Don Quixote in England (1734), The In-
triguing Chambermaid (1734), and The Author's Farce (1730).
Almost no play entirely omits one or the other of these plot
elements; however, those which are predominantly political
satires (like Pasquin (1736) and The Historical Register (1737)
and burlesque (like Tom Thumb) [1730] and Covent Garden
Tragedy [1732]) provide little more than occasional witticism
on love and marriage.

tle influence of moralizing tendencies. The comedies reveal
in varying degrees the infiltration of sentimental attitudes.
Only The Modern Husband is a departure of sufficient importance to merit separate consideration. On this play Fielding
lavished a great deal of effort, and his comments about it indicate that he felt himself to be writing on a model not attempted before; C.B. Woods labels it a comedy of overt social
purpose.[10]

All of Fielding's comedies reflect the world of Restoration
conventions. In that world as portrayed in comedy, "the pursuit of women was the principal business of life...marriage
was the most dreaded calamity, and that love was strong indeed
which would submit to it" for any but mercenary motives.[11]
As the rake in The Universal Gallant puts it, the whole pleasure of life is the pursuit; the pleasure ends simultaneously
with the chase. The pursuit, or courtship, is regarded as a
time when any deception is expected and is permissible, the
more so if marriage is to be the end of the game. In case the
players are already married, any intrigue is laudable which
promotes the gaining of a new mistress or the cuckolding of a
gullible husband. The degree of popular cynicism toward the
institution of marriage is constantly echoed throughout Fielding's comedies. Young Owen, a suitor in The Grub Street
Opera, declares that marriage is "a dirty road to love—and
those are happiest who arrive at love without travelling through
it" (II, ii). Sir Positive Trap, the guardian uncle in Fielding's
earliest play, Love in Several Masques, equates marriage
with being "wedded, bedded, and executed" (II, vi).

The only acknowledged motive for surrender to marriage
is gain; the negotiations are the business of coldly calculating
guardians who wish to make the best of their marketable mer-
chandise. Again Sir Positive Trap sums up the main concern
of guardians in his questioning of a suitor for his niece:

Where's your estate, sir? what's your title, sir? what's
your coat of arms? Does your estate lie in terra firma,
or in stocks? (V, vi)

To his niece's protests against his prerogative in arranging a
match, Sir Positive Trap declares

I never saw my lady there till an hour before our marriage. I made my addresses to her father, her father to
his lawyer, the lawyer to my estate...the bargain was
struck...what need have young people of addressing, or
anything, till they come to undressing? (II, vi)

Furthermore, he tells her,it is his hope "to see the time when
a man may carry his daughter to market with the same lawful
authority as any other of his cattle."

The predicament of children of such parents or guardians
is clear in a scene between Young Pedant and his father in The
Temple Beau. The son objects first to matrimony itself, second to the person, his cousin. The father replies, "If you refuse, I'll disinherit you." Young Pedant, his own motives none
too pure, admits his father's is a "substantial, prevalent, and
convincing argument" (I, iii). To the charge that Bellaria's
principles are not fit for a wife, Sir Avarice Pedant declares
to his son that "she has twenty thousand pounds—very good
principles." Moreover, if he were to receive "a pound for
every flaw, the more she had, the better" (IV, iii). The conniving mother in The Grub Street Opera assures her daughter
that "no qualities can make amends for the want of fortune, and
that fortune makes a sufficient amends for the want of every
good quality" (II, i).

It is a natural step from such motivation to its inevitable
consequences. One of the rules of fashionable behavior among
married couples was, even in the rare instance of true affection, never to reveal in public any concern for a mate. (See
Appendix C.) Better yet if the indifference or hatred were
real. Lady Lucy (TB) describes the age as one "when 'tis as
immodest to love before marriage, as 'tis unfashionable to
love after it" (II, vii). Apish Simple, the fop in Love in Several Masques, assures Helena that they will be a thoroughly
fashionable couple who will "hate one another with as good-
breeding as any couple under the sun" (V, iii).

In a sprightly scene between Lucy, the hoydenish heiress,
and one of her suitors, Blister, in An Old Man Taught Wisdom;
or, The Virgin Unmasked, Fielding exploited the opportunity

for satirizing the fashionable society which Lucy longs to be a part of and in so doing combined a number of motifs common to the plays: the general low esteem of the married state, the mutual dislike of the partners, and their accepted infidelity to each other.

> Blister: ...as for liking me, do not give yourself any trouble about that, it is the very best reason for marrying me...hating one another is the chief end of matrimony....I fancy you have not a right notion of married life. I suppose you imagine we are to be fond, and kiss and hug one another as long as we live.
>
> Lucy: Why, an't we?
>
> Blister: ...Marrying is nothing but living in the same house together, and going by the same name; while I am following my business, you will be following your pleasure; so that we shall rarely meet but at meals, and then we are to sit at opposite ends of the table, and make faces at each other.
>
> Lucy: Ah, but there is one thing though—an't we to lie together?
>
> Blister: A fortnight, no longer.
>
> Lucy: A fortnight! That's a long time; but it will be over.
>
> Blister: Ay, and then you may have anyone else.
>
> Lucy: May I? Then...by Goles! Why this is pure.
> (I, iv)

Such infidelity as Lucy anticipates is the central subject of the plays of the second type, the married-love intrigues. Fielding's early farce The Letter Writers exemplifies the type. The farce turns on the efforts of two older husbands to keep their young wives at home by writing anonymous letters threatening to murder them if they stir abroad. The wives react in opposite fashion. Mrs. Wisdom stays at home; Mrs. Softly hires extra footmen to serve as guards and goes out all

the more to show her courage. Neither is hindered in her intrigues with Rakel, the paramour of both ladies. The action of
the play consists of skirmishes between the husbands and the
gallant, who declares that he has been at "war with the whole
commonwealth of husbands" since he reached the age of discretion (I, xi). The gulled husbands are "cits," the cuckolded-
merchant husbands familiar in early Restoration comedy.[12]
Their concern for their wives' fidelity is exceeded only by
their zeal for executing profitable business deals. The play
ends with the husbands the victims of ridicule; by implication
at least, they are two old fools who deserve to be deceived.
Moreover, they suffer the further indignity of being lectured
by Rakel not "by any force or sinister stratagem to imprison
... [their] wives. The laws of England are too generous to
permit the one, and the ladies are generally too cunning to be
outwitted by the other" (III, x). The typical Restoration "moral" sums up the rake's triumph:

> Those wives for pleasures very seldom roam
> Whose husbands bring substantial pleasures home.

There is no condemnation of the infidelity of the wives. The
only chastisement of either the wives or the rake is the post-
poning of their anticipated pleasures. There is, in fact, nothing in the play to suggest any more serious aim on Fielding's
part than to put together a profitable entertainment based on
time-tested subject matter—the unsuccessful devices of old
men in farcical literature for securing the young wives they
have bought.

Flagrant disregard of fidelity in marriage is described by
Sir Simon Raffler in The Universal Gallant; there is nothing
but cuckoldom everywhere. He daily expects to see "an article
in the newspapers, and 'Cuckolds since our last list' as regularly inserted as bankrupts are now" (I, i). Obsessed with the
fear of being cuckolded, he describes the sorry lot of husbands:

> If a husband had a hundred thousand eyes, he would have
> use for them all. A wife is a garrison without walls,

> while we are running to the defence of one quarter, she
> is taken at another.... One goes to work with his purse,
> and buys my wife; a second brings his title.... A third
> shows a garter, a fourth a smooth face, another a smooth
> tongue... this sings, that dances... in short, all her five
> senses, and five thousand follies, have their addressers
> (V, i).

Even the rake protests that women are growing so inconstant
that soon a gallant will be no more able to keep a woman to
himself than her husband can (I, i). It is so civil and com-
municative an age, he complains, that it is no more a breach
of friendship to make use of man's wife than of his chariot.

Courtship leading to matrimony based on such motives and
characterized by infidelity could hardly have differed from
marriage in its basic nature. Lady Trap denounces it as "an
abominable, diabolical practice and the parent of nothing but
lies and flattery" (LISM, I, vi). Deception was expected,
whether in claims of rank and fortune or vows of love. Lady
Matchless declares that "courtship is to marriage like a fine
avenue to an old falling manion beautified with a painted front."
(LISM, III, v). With so little substance of love to hope for after marriage, a woman required much show of it before marriage. It was her obligation to encourage lovers in order to
make fools of mankind. Her wit and beauty were weapons to
enslave men. Her eyes should conquer the world and weep,
like Alexander's, for more worlds to conquer (TB, II, vii).
Bellaria mockingly prescribes the fashionable courtship of the
day to a suitor she despises:

> You must flatter me egregiously; not only with more
> perfections than I have, but than ever any one had; for
> which you must submit to very ill usage. And when I
> have treated you like a tyrant overnight, you must, in a
> submissive letter, ask my pardon the next morning, for
> having offended me: though you have done nothing... You
> must follow me to all public places where I shall give an
> unlimited encouragement to the most notorious fools I

can meet with, at which you are to seem very much concerned, but not dare to upbraid me with it—then...you
are sometimes to be honoured with playing with me at
quadrille; where, to show you my good-nature, I will
take as much of your money as I can possibly cheat you
of. And when you have done all these, and twenty more
such trifling things, for one five years, I shall be convinced—that you are an ass, and laugh at you five times
more heartily than I do now (TB, V, vi).

A suitor was judged by his appearance and his adeptness at
wooing according to rule, fashionable courtship being ideally a
war of wit. If the lovers surrender to the force of love, they
maintain a pose of raillery and typically set up terms for their
marriage which, if carried out, will allow them the freedom
to move from the maneuvers of courtship to the real battle of
married intrigue. Lady Matchless objects to a sensible suitor,
Wisemore, because he lacks this kind of wit and "stumbles at
every straw we throw in his way, which a fop would skip over
with ease" (LISM, II, i).

As the examples cited indicate, there are numerous evidences in Fielding's plays of Restoration cynicism concerning
marriage as a business venture requiring neither the love nor
constancy of the partners, and courtship as a time of dissimulation. However, Fielding usually puts these comments in the
mouths of characters who are themselves the object of satire
(as the pedant, the fop, the hoyden) or whose comments have
satiric intent. Although his condemnations of the follies of
courtship and marriage are usually, and properly for a satirist, made in this manner, he was on occasion openly didactic,
using exemplary characters to make a straightforward protest.

One of the strongest points which Fielding makes consistently throughout the comedies is his insistence that the only
satisfactory basis for marriage is love and merit. In Love in
Several Masques, Helena objects to being "put up at auction!
to be disposed, as a piece of goods, by way of bargain and
sale" (II, v). Her own choice, she insists, will be a man whose
merit is his only wealth. Wisemore in the same play declares

that his heart is not "a place of mercenary entertainment."
The only title to a woman's love should be based on "merit,
love, and constancy" (IV, ii). Bellaria, in The Temple Beau,
like Helena, insists that merit is the basis of love. Veromil
matches her idealistic sentiments, for his love for her is based
on diviner excellencies of the mind and their linked souls (IV,
x). In The Fathers, which of all Fielding's plays shows the
strongest influence of the sentimental movement, the good-
natured father agrees with his son that choosing the marriage
partner is a power usurped in a parent. However, he cautions
his son to remember that the child is guided primarily by the
desire to satisfy an immediate passion, while the parent looks
forward to future happiness (II, i). To the proposal of Sir
Gregory Kennel, who is concerned only with monetary advantage, that the wedding take place between his son and Miss
Boncour immediately upon the settling of the terms, the uncle
protests with feeling, "Do you think that a union of bodies is
all that is requisite in a state wherein there can be no happiness without a union of minds too?" (V, 5)

The partners in an idealized courtship or marriage in
Fielding's plays are not usually typical Restoration lovers of
the tradition of the gay couple. Actually the decline of this
type was already well underway in the 1690's. There had always existed even within the society portrayed in Restoration
comedy a consciousness of a double standard.[13] Somewhere
in the midst of the assortment of worldly characters was a
young girl, however skillful in the art of raillery, whose virtue was not in question. Her lover, whatever his past, had at
least temporarily redeemed himself by his sincere love. In
post-1700 comedy, "the young people who approach love with
reverence are better thought of than those who speak of it with
seeming flippancy."[14] One or both partners have become converted to good sense. Often the witty heroine uses the serious
lover as the butt for her wit, e.g. Lady Matchless, but is finally converted by the man of sense, in this case, Wisemore
(LISM). Heartfort, in The Wedding Day, faces a similar obstacle in winning the perverse Charlotte. Occasionally there
is a lively hero who must be chastened by a serious heroine.

Gaylove in <u>The Universal Gallant</u> has become a sensible lover
but is not so thoroughly reformed as to be averse to a little
love intrigue. The careless lover lingers on, as Gaylove illustrates, but "happy the gallant who, sensing the temper of
the times, has reformed his life and become an honest lover
intent on matrimony—in other words, a man of sense—by the
time the play begins."[15] Fielding frequently uses this admirable couple of good sense; significantly, however, they regularly play a secondary role. The chief interest lies elsewhere.

With the increasing prominence of the sensible lovers there
is a corresponding change in courtship. The wit duel is at
least balanced by scenes of open profession of love. Unlike
her Restoration sisters, the woman of sense, whether sweetheart or wife, is quick to forgive, as Bellaria does Veromil's
unwarranted jealousy (<u>TB</u>, III, xii) and as Mrs. Bellamant
does her husband's infidelity (<u>MH</u>, IV, x).

Much of Fielding's didacticism bears overtones of the sentimental attitudes which were well established by the time he
wrote. The great era of the sentimental comedy coincided exactly with his most successful years as a dramatist, the 1730's.
The use of exemplary characters is but one instance of this
influence. The strongest tenet of sentimental comedy was that
virtue must be rewarded and vice punished or at least reformed. There are a few examples in Fielding's plays of
reformation that should have warmed the hearts of the strongest moralists. Fielding makes use of the favorite device of a
noble friend, or sweetheart, who serves as the instrument of
salvation. In a thoroughly sentimental scene in <u>The Temple
Beau</u>, Veromil appeals to his friend Valentine on the basis of
his essential goodness and reason to give up his pursuit of
Bellaria, which is motivated by physical desire. Veromil assures the repentant Valentine that "the perfect joy that flows
from the reflection of a virtuous deed far surpasses all the
trifling momentary raptures that are obtained by guilt" (IV,x)
—an aphorism to melt the heart of Steele!

An interesting example of the fifth-act conversion against
which Fielding was later to protest in <u>Tom Jones</u> (VIII, i) occurs in the reform of the libertine in <u>The Wedding Day</u>. Mil-

amour, having lost his lady to a wealthy old husband, plans to gain her as his mistress. His friend Heartfort reasons with him

Heartfort: What privilege does thou perceive in thyself to invade and destroy the happiness of another? Besides, though shame may first reach the husband, it doth not always end there; the wife is always liable, and often is involved in the ruin of the gallant. The person who deserves chiefly to be exposed to shame is the only person who escapes without it....I know ...that what thou dost of this kind arises from thy not considering the consequences of thy actions; and if any woman can lay her ruin on thee, thou canst lay it on custom.

Millamour: Why, indeed, if we consider it in a serious way—

Heartfort: And why should we not? Custom may lead a man into many errors, but it justifies none ...in reality, there is no more mischievous character than a public debaucher of women.

Millamour: No more, dear George; now you begin to pierce to the quick.

Heartfort: I have done. I am glad you can feel; it is a sure sign of no mortification.

Millamour: Yes, I can feel, and too much, that I have been in the wrong to a woman, who hath no fault but foolishly loving me. 'Sdeath! thou hast raised a devil in me that will sufficiently revenge her quarrel. Oh! Heartfort, how was it possible for me to be guilty of so much barbarity without knowing it, and of doing her so many wrongs without seeing them till this moment, till it is too late, till I can make her no reparation (V, iii)?

Consistent with the sentimental reward of reformation, he

can and does make reparation: Clarinda is restored to him,
and he assures her

> [My] former follies may, through an excess of good for-
> tune, prove advantageous to both in our future happiness.
> While I, from the reflection on the danger of losing you
> ...shall enjoy the bliss with doubled sweetness;...you
> from thence may derive a tender and constant husband
> (V, xii).

Interestingly enough, this is exactly the reasoning in Pamela
for the conversion of Mr. B—into a model husband which was
to arouse Fielding's highest genius in parody.

One aspect of the moralized comedy is almost entirely ab-
sent from Fielding's plays; that is the tendency to idealize
members of the lower and middle-class characters, especially
the merchant, who had suffered as the "cit" at the hands of
Restoration writers, and continued to do so well into the eighteenth century. Even Defoe, himself struggling to rise from
this class, has Moll Flanders describe one of her husbands
with considerable scorn as an "amphibious creature, this
land-water thing," a gentleman-tradesman. In only one play
does Fielding make a decided statement for the worth of a
servant-suitor. The giddy Lucy of An Old Man Taught Wisdom
defies her father's plans and elopes with the footman, Thomas.
He answers objections to his station with a ringing declaration
of his worth.

> Your daughter has married a man of some learning, and
> one who has seen a little of the world, and who by his
> love to her, and obedience to you, will try to deserve
> your favours...as I have lived in a great family I have
> seen that no one is respected for what he is, but for what
> he has; the world pays no regard at present to anything
> but money; and if my own industry should add to your
> fortune, so as to entitle any of my posterity to grandeur,
> it will be no reason against making my son, or grandson,
> a lord, that his father, or grandfather, was a footman
> (I, xi).

It is noteworthy that he is expressing the favorite dream of the eighteenth-century middle class man—to rise in the social scale and to see one's son a gentleman, even a lord! However, the effect of this statement is offset by Lucy's reasons for preferring him, which have more to do with his pretty curls, well-shaped legs, and physical prowess than his innate merit.

There are throughout the marriage plays, from the earliest to the last, evidences of idealization of courtship, love, and marriage and the consciousness of false values and the ruin resulting from them. Whether they can be simply equated with the sentimental is debatable, as protests against such false standards can be found all through the Restoration period proper. One need cite only Wycherley among the most successful of the Restoration dramatists for evidence of this protest. Moreover, it is easy to distort the importance of these elements by the simple enumeration of them. The final test of a play is its total effect. There are exemplary characters who speak out against the follies and vices of custom, but it is rather the parade of types already familiar from the older comedy that remains in the mind—coquettes, rakes, fops, gulled husbands, faithless wives, superannuated beauties, prudes—many of them to reappear later in the novels. Moreover, the society in which they exist is a cynical one motivated by greed and selfish desires, not an idyllic one in which happiness crowns virtue, constancy, and love. In only two plays, The Wedding Day and The Fathers, is the sentimental strain really strong. Interestingly, neither of these was staged during the period of Fielding's career as a dramatist. The Wedding Day was presented in 1743; The Fathers, not until 1778, almost twenty-five years after Fielding's death. In most of the comedies all ends well with the various, but not necessarily deserving, lovers without any great adjustment in their basic philosophy. Successful stratagems have extricated them from predicaments or luck has favored them. Fielding's condemnation of this society must rest on the unloveliness of the characters who exemplify the follies and vices he despises, not on wholesale reformation of erring characters whose repentance is followed by appropriate rewards. P. F. Vernon, in

a study of Restoration comedy, sees in the satiric portrait of
marriage an implicit and consistent moral purpose.[16] Fielding said as much in his own defense against a critic who
charged him with recommending immorality, specifically
whoring and drunkenness: "How! Why a rake speaks against
matrimony, and a sot against sobriety."

Fielding made his most outspoken criticism of contemporary vice in The Modern Husband (1732), which deserves special
attention not only because of its comments on marriage but
also because of its striking resemblance to Amelia. Dobson
dismissed The Modern Husband as hardly creditable to Fielding's artistic or moral sense because it dealt with the "most
loathsome of commercial pursuits, the traffic of a husband in
his wife's dishonour."[17] Dobson consequently found Fielding's
"complacency" regarding the play odd. Cross recognized that
Fielding's attitude was not one of complacency but of special
concern for a work which seems to have been longer in preparation than any other of his plays. It had circulated in manu-
script among his friends for more than a year before Fielding
submitted it to his cousin, Lady Mary Wortley Montagu. He
described it to her as "written on a Model...never yet attempted." Cross interprets the new model to mean that it was
"neither farce nor a Congreve wit-trap, but a serious comedy
representing...certain phases of contemporary life." Cross
further questions whether the play can accurately be considered a comedy at all. He calls it a "novel in dramatic form
running through five acts to eighty-odd pages of prose."[18]

Charles Woods offers the first challenge to these generally
accepted views of the play.[19] He cites the fourteen perform-
ances as anything but the run of a failure. Moreover, a contemporary reviewer refers to "the favorable reception The
Modern Husband has met with." The heart of Woods' study is
an attempt to establish the source of the play in a contemporary lawsuit which exactly parallels the events in the play.
Fielding's purpose, he believes, is more than the censure of
private vice; it is rather an attempt to reform the law, which
allowed connivance between husband and wife to get damages
from a defendant. Thus, Fielding is accurately describing

his play as written on a new model, comedy as a vehicle for social criticism with the aim of amending the law itself.

Woods points out the serious intent stated in the prologue of the play: the author is repenting "frolic flights of youth, i. e. farce and burlesque, and returning to "nature and the truth" in order to "divert, instruct, and mend mankind." There is, however, some support of the tradition that Fielding considered the reception of the play as disappointing, and certainly proof that the prologue cannot be taken literally, in the fact that he did not follow up this effort as a censor of morals with another play in a similar vein. In fact, his next production was a relapse into those very frolic flights he avowed he was repenting of, The Covent Garden Tragedy, a bawdy burlesque of The Distrest Mother.

The Modern Husband presents the story of "a willing cuckold who sells his willing wife." The Moderns are contrasted with the Bellamants, who up to the events of the play, have been a happily married pair. Bellamant, despite his sincere love for his wife, has become involved in an affair with Mrs. Modern which threatens his marriage. Driven by the urgencies of extravagant living, Mr. Modern proposes as a solution to their present straits that Mrs. Modern allow herself to be discovered with her lover, Lord Richly. The following scene is typical of the offensive nature of the subject matter and the tone of the play as a whole.

Mr. M.	Your person is mine: I bought it lawfully in the church; and unless I am to profit by the disposal, I shall keep it all for my own use .... Have I not winked at all your intrigues? Have I not pretended business, to leave you and your gallants together? Have I not been the most obsequious, observant--
Mrs. M.	Out with it; you know what you are.
Mr. M.	Do you upbraid me with your vices, madam?
Mrs. M.	...Call it obedience to a husband's will. Can you deny that you have yourself persuaded me to the undertaking? Can you forget the

	arguments you used to convince me that virtue was the lightest of bubbles?
Mr. M.	I own it all...but, as I must more than share the dishonour, it is surely reasonable that I should share the profit.
Mrs. M.	And have you not?....Why do you complain then?
Mr. M.	Because I find those effects no more.... In short, it is impossible that your amours should be secret long; and however careless you have been of me whilst I had my horns in my pocket, I hope you'll take care to gild them when I am to wear them in public.
Mrs. M.	What would you have me do?
Mr. M.	Suffer me to discover you together; by which means we may make our fortunes easy all at once. One good discovery in Westminster Hall will be of greater service than his utmost generosity—The law will give you more in one moment, than his love for many years (IV, i).

As despicable as the pimping husband, is the abandoned libertine, Lord Richly. He proposes to use his cast-off mistress, Mrs. Modern, as his bawd in arranging a new alliance, this time with Mrs. Bellamant. He tells Mrs. Modern that when "a man is to lay out his money, he is always to do it with his friends" (II, vii). He takes pride in the purchase of his mistresses. He assures his nephew that marriage to a girl whose father is impoverished is unnecessary, "for poverty as surely brings a woman to capitulation, as scarcity of provision does a garrison" (V, vii). Assuming that Mrs. Bellamant also has a price, he suggests that she make her husband's fortune by the sale of herself, a method used by half the ladies of the town.

When Mrs. Modern is convinced that she can get nothing from Lord Richly, she seeks money from her new lover, Bellamant. Modern goes ahead with his plan to discover his wife,

but it is Bellamant, not Richly, whom he surprises. Bellamant's infidelity is forgiven by the generous Mrs. Bellamant;
the Moderns and Richly receive their just deserts.

The play, in spite of a fourteen-night run, seems not to
have pleased either those who came for diversion or those who
sought instruction. It drew hisses from the audiences, for the
harmless characters as well as the vicious. The explanation
of the play's reception is hardly the offensiveness of its subject matter alone, for infidelity was a theme familiar on the
stage. Apparently it did not please those with a taste for Restoration comedy because it did not serve up infidelity with the
usual spice. There is little of gaiety and wit in the whole play.
The characters are for the most part vicious or loathsome
rather than ridiculous. They arouse disgust rather than laughter. The only pleasant characters in the play were hissed
along with the Moderns and Richly. Charlotte Gaywit, a
feather-brained young girl, works diligently to fulfill her ideas
of what a fashionable woman is. She is, in spite of her silli-
ness, a good-natured girl of sound character. She is simply
a Restoration butterfly fluttering in the wrong garden. Young
Bellamant, her lover, is an apt protagonist in the wit duels
which eventually trap them, willingly, in marriage. The contrast between their harmless frivolity and the depravity of the
major characters increases the unpleasantness of the effect of
the play. However, such a strong reaction against these two
suggests a changing taste in the audience.

What Woods calls a large amount of "more or less extrane-
ous material, which shows the influence of sentimental dramatists," was no doubt woven into the play to please that portion
of the audience which favored the moralized comedy. The
sensible couple, Lord Richly's nephew Gaywit and the Bellamants' daughter Emilia, offer a sober courtship full of eloquent testimonials to highmindedness. However, Gaywit's
stature as an exemplary lover is somewhat diminished by the
revelation that he too is a former lover of Mrs. Modern's.
The moralists should have exulted in the triumph of the virtuous Mrs. Bellamant, the repentance of Bellamant, and the
punishment of the Moderns and Richly; perhaps the sordidness

of the scenes of trade were too strong. Moreover, the appeal
to pity made for Mrs. Modern as a "woman whose faults are
more her husband's than her own" fails because the audience
has seen her as much sinning as sinned against. She is, or
has been, engaged in illicit affairs with every important male
character in the play except young Bellamant.

Fielding's special interest in this play and the sincerity of
his efforts are clear in the fuller development of the characters and situations twenty years later in Amelia. The novel
even bears the name of the exemplary young Emilia Bellamant.
The similarities between the play and the novel are obvious.
Mrs. Bellamant becomes Amelia in the novel; Bellamant's
affair with Mrs. Modern parallels that of Booth and Miss Matthews. The pimping husband appears as Captain Trent, and
various shades of Lord Richly are presented in the rich unnamed gentleman and in Booth's friend Colonel James. Even
subordinate themes, like the failure of Merit, a deserving soldier, are incorporated in the difficulties of Booth.

The Modern Husband is forceful evidence in Fielding's
dramatic career of his awareness at a very young age, of the
terrible consequences of violation of laws of morality in marriage. Its savage indictment of the fashions of the age as a
contributing factor was not to be matched by anything he wrote
until Amelia. That it came so early and was not followed by
plays which reveal a consistent approach and a deepening seriousness is proof only that Fielding was a popular playwright,
not a social crusader. It makes clear the insight of George
Bernard Shaw when he called Fielding the "greatest practicing
dramatist, with the single exception of Shakespeare, produced
by England between the Middle Ages and the nineteenth century." He was writing for immediate production; he wrote to
suit his audiences. If he failed, he revised or produced a new
play, often in a matter of a few hours. There is some literal
truth in his description of his choice of a career as a dramatist as "hackney writer." The quality of his work varies from
play to play as remarkably as does the earnestness of the
message. There is no reason to quarrel with Fielding's own
often-quoted estimate of his dramatic productions, "that he

left off writing for the stage, when he ought to have begun."

Much of Fielding's acceptance of Restoration attitudes toward marriage and related problems was simply the novice's use of popular conventions, tested and proven successful as material for the stage. There is no doubt that his inclination toward idealization of marriage was strong from the first play to the last. This inclination was to be crystallized by Pamela, that ultimate expression, in Fielding's judgment, of false values as the basis of marriage. The morality of Pamela, with gold as its standard, is quite in harmony with the mercenary motives portrayed in Restoration comedy. Fielding himself had been content to utilize the conventional money-grabbing heroine in his comedies; but when pretense entered and the calculating girl palmed herself off as virtuous, she was reprehensible to him. The obvious unrealism of the plays, except The Modern Husband, generally left Fielding with a set of tricks to pull, not with a group of seriously realistic characters to develop.

In the novels Fielding moves steadily in the direction of the illusion of actuality. His conscious pose as a historian is part of this effort. The two earlier novels, Jonathan Wild and Joseph Andrews, do indeed have much of life and human nature accurately portrayed, but their real vitality depends on an intellectual exercise in irony and parody. The reader must be constantly alert to catch the various levels of meaning. Much of the discussion of the character of Joseph centers around the intrusion into the parody element of what may be termed actuality, as Joseph ceases to be a figure of mere parody. In Tom Jones and Amelia the emphasis on actuality dominates; elements of burlesque and irony are still frequently present in Tom Jones, but they are almost entirely lacking in Amelia. One may see that the characters grow in realism; and as Fielding progresses toward the creation of a world closely approximating the actual, he also moves away from the broad farcical techniques of his early work. The full force of Fielding's growth from a boisterous relish for life and tolerance of the foibles and failings of the human race to an intense concern for the welfare of his fellow man is the most impressive effect of viewing his career in its entirety.

If there is no consistent growth in technique and treatment of subject matter in the plays as a single segment of his career, there is, on the other hand, evidence from the beginning of the serious attitude toward marriage which Fielding was to treat fully in the novels.

Chapter 3

MARRIAGE IN THE EARLY NOVELS

Fielding ended his dramatic career in 1737, as he had begun it nine years earlier, predominantly a Restoration playwright in choice of subject matter and manner of treatment. In dealing with courtship and marriage, he still reflected the cynicism of his models; his advocacy of marriage based on love and merit was balanced by repeated use of Restoration conventions. His plays offer evidence that he saw clearly enough the injustices and disastrous consequences of marriage arranged on mercenary considerations alone and of the general contempt directed at marriage, but he was no crusader for matrimonial reform.

The publication of Pamela (1740) provided the impetus for Fielding's real genius as a writer, genius that found its expression in the novel rather than in the drama. Fielding's indignation on both moral and artistic grounds was aroused by what he considered the glorification of hypocrisy under the name of virtue. The first result was Shamela (1741), which aimed its satire at both the form and substance of Pamela, and a year later, Joseph Andrews, which goes far beyond mere parody of Pamela.

The "phrenzical" success of Pamela, as Fielding disparagingly dubbed it, no doubt resulted from its gratification of the desires of its audience. Literature of and about the lower and middle classes had always existed at least on the subliterary level in the oral fabliaux and in a rich body of Renaissance stories of the picaresque tradition. Defoe in the early years of the century added to the picaresque formula the element of financial success for his heroes and heroines, but he failed to give them the last ingredient dear to the heart of the rising

middle class—true respectability. No matter how prosperous
Moll and Roxanne might grow, their shady past clung about
them. Pamela,. however, was clothed in respectability and
religious piety to suit the puritanic taste of the day.

As a commentary on marriage, Pamela can be summed up
as commending two cardinal tenets. From a woman's point of
view, virtue (that is, virginity) is a marketable commodity to
be zealously guarded until sale (that is, marriage) is arranged
with the highest bidder. From a man's point of view, marriage
is a last extremity to be entered into only if enjoyment of the
desired object is impossible by other means. In short, mercenary motives and lust are the foundations of the marriage
between Pamela and Mr. B__. Richardson declares the result of this match between a scheming opportunist and a reformed rake to be matrimonial bliss and harmony. Richardson's sincerity in offering Pamela as a moral book and his
unawareness of any inadequacy in his heroine's moral values
testify to his own acceptance of a set of values completely an-
tipathetic to Fielding. Ernest A. Baker describes the Fleet
Street printer as "himself Pamela, heart and soul, as he wrote
her letters."[20] For Richardson, and thus for Pamela, there
were two absolute requisites for success in marriage: the
marriage must raise the social level of the woman, and the
bride must come to the marriage bed a virgin.

Richardson was expressing the convictions of many of his
contemporaries, as well as his own, when he linked chastity
and economic motives. As Ian Watt points out, Pamela was
written at a time when the older patriarchal family order was
being supplanted by the conjugal family, that is, each married
pair set up independently, often far from the parents, as an
autonomous unit economically and socially.[21] The changing
economic situation in the century and its effect on the position
of women is the chief factor behind the love plot with economic
obstacles, which was the mainstay of the English novel.

By the beginning of the eighteenth century the capitalistic
organization of industry on an individual basis had ad-
vanced so far as to free men from much of their eco-

nomic dependence on their wives, and the woman's economic value was lessened. [22]

There was heightened interest in the struggle of women in this increasingly individualistic social order to obtain status by their own free choice of a mate. Steele described the problem in <u>The Tender Husband</u>: marriageable girls, he says, are a drug on the market. Because of wars and colonization, which were reducing the numbers of men at the very time when the "value" of a wife was lessened, husbands were scarce even for girls with an adequate dowry. The only ways wide open to women were marriage and prostitution. They might take their dowry (the sex function) "to the Exchange, which was marriage, or play it on the Curb, which was prostitution."[23] If a woman chose neither of these courses, she added one more to a growing class, dependent maiden ladies, obnoxious to their relatives because they were no longer valuable as contributing members to a domestic economy.

It is exactly this situation which Defoe's Moll Flanders rails against:

[The men] insult us mightily with telling us of the number of women; that the wars, and the sea, and trade, and other incidents have carried the men so much away, that there is no proportion between the numbers of the sexes, and therefore the women have the disadvantage.

Moll, however, declares that the advantage is not so much on the other side as the men think it is

and though it may be true that the men have but too much choice among us, and that some women may be found who will dishonour themselves, be cheap, and easy to come at, and will scarce wait to be asked, yet if they will have women...worth having, they may find them as uncome-atable as ever.

Moll's final advice is directed particularly to those women

having some dowry; they may certainly exercise great caution, lest they be victims of fortune hunters.

This social change in the pattern of family life with its allied change in a woman's position was occurring simultaneously with "a tremendous narrowing of the ethical scale, a redefinition of virtue in primarly sexual terms."[24] Virtue was being more and more equated with chastity, and the economic significance of chastity is clearly stated in Samuel Johnson's comment that upon the woman's chastity, "all the property in the world depends."[25] A.R. Wagner in English Ancestry approaches the matter in terms of the number of heirs among whom property must be divided. Thus, since a small number of recipients receive large shares per capita, both female chastity and improved health measures, with lower infant mortality, became matters of grave concern in a stable economy. Maintaining family status paradoxically requires small families.[26]

William M. Sale, Jr. attributes Richardson's great appeal to his own generation to his attempt to interpret the vital social problem of "interpenetration of the emergent middle class and the surviving aristocracy." In choosing heroines who sought union with, not opposition to, social superiors who threaten their integrity, Richardson unites a number of issues of great appeal.[27] Complicating the heroines' struggles is the fact that they strive to preserve that integrity, which for Richardson was represented by the symbol of chastity.

Richardson's emphasis upon his heroines' fascination with every detail of marriage and an "equally striking horror of any sexual advance or reference until the conjugal knot is tied" can be explained, Watt believes, as the result of the assimilation of values of romantic love to spiritually idealized marriage in the Puritan concept.[28] A decisive force in Richardson's success in fusing these divergent views of love is the theologically charged language in which the heroine's struggle is described. The contemporary audience was well prepared for what Bell calls the "submerged stream of Christian symbolism" which, for example, permeates the dialogue between Pamela and Mr. B__ and Pamela's meditations as well. Rich-

ardson's rich ambiguity of religious and secular language satisfied the desire for romantic experience sanctioned by religious terminology.

The Puritan viewed sexual activity outside marriage as
sinful and condemned extramarital alliances, which, though
never publicly approved, had traditionally been accepted as
inevitable in a system of marriage for convenience. The middle class exhibited the greatest zeal in espousing the tenet of
chastity and marriage combining practical motives and romantic love, as it had sanctioned the association of chastity
with economic motives. Richardson was of this class, as was
the bulk of his audience. In Pamela, he epitomized the excellencies dearest to the middle-class Puritan mind.[29] The ideal
is a young, inexperienced girl so delicate in physical and
mental constitution that she swoons at any sexual advance.
Essentially a passive creature, she exhibits little feeling, except perhaps fear, for her suitor until the marriage is effected. Chastity is her highest virtue; her reward, marriage
which elevates her socially. It was this restriction and per-
version of the term virtue to mean chastity, with overtones of
barter and sale, which was offensive to Fielding.

Fielding was not by birth of the middle class; hence he did
not share the aspirations of this group for social elevation by
marriage. Moreover, his religious and moral outlook was not
as restricted as Richardson's. Fielding regarded virtue as a
natural tendency to goodness or benevolence rather than the
result of suppression of instinct (Tom Jones, III, 2-7). The
difference in the authors' attitudes is immediately obvious in
the heroines they present. No Richardson heroine could marry "down"; he states the case explicitly in the quarrel between
Lady Davers and Mr. B__ over his marriage to an inferior.
Lady Davers can see no difference between a beggar's son
married by a lady and a beggar's daughter made a gentleman's
wife. Mr. B__ enlightens her thus:

the difference is, a man ennobles the woman he takes, be
she who she will; and adopts her into his own rank, be
it what it will; but a woman, though ever so nobly born,

debases herself by a mean marriage and descends from
her own rank to his she stoops to. [30]

Fielding's Sophia and Amelia, by contrast with Richardson's
heroines, do marry down. Their aim, unlike Pamela's, is not
colored by the ambition to advance themselves socially or
economically. Tom's lack of wealth is of course only a temporary obstacle; Booth, however, remains beneath Amelia and
it is her regained inheritance which solves their financial difficulties. The further divergence of Fielding's heroines from
the Pamela-pattern will be discussed in more detail in subsequent chapters.

The heart of Fielding's parody in Shamela is the exposing
of the true nature of the sentiments and motives of Pamela,
motives which, according to Fielding's view of life, are contemptible and at last destructive. By setting Shamela beside
Pamela, Fielding is exposing a single character "in two sets
of dress—or if you will, undress." The seeming contradictions
between the two begin to disappear. Pamela's morality, no
less than Shamela's, has gold for its standard. "Pamela knows
full well that she carries a jewel on her person; and the best
that can be said for her is that once she has established a
price for her jewel no one can talk her into lowering it." [31]

All of Pamela's actions become logical in the light of busi-
ness-like calculation of Mr. B__'s passion. She lingers to em-
broider her master's waistcoat in order to keep her charms
visible should his ardor diminish. She repeatedly delays her
departure on any pretext; and once she is on her way, her
master has only to send her news of his surrender—he will
marry her—and she is so hasty in her return to seal the bargain that she taxes the endurance of both the coach driver and
the horses.

The most offensive quality of Pamela's behavior, however,
is not her willingness to accept without hesitation a man whom
she has consistently declared beyond her station and whose
courtship of her Kreissman summarizes as "revilement, in-
carceration, kidnaping, and attempted rape." It is her servile
gratitude for his condescension to marry her. After Mr. B__

assures Pamela he can "joyfully subscribe" to all conditions
of the actual marriage service, Pamela writes: "I kissed his
dear hand: O my generous, kind protector...how gracious is
it to confirm the doubting mind of your poor servant! which
apprehends nothing so much as her unworthiness of the honour
and blessing that await her!" And at the ceremony itself, upon
receiving the ring, Pamela curtsies and says, "Thank you,
sir." Her subservience is the more objectionable when one
considers Mr. B__. There is no charity sufficient to clothe
him in other than his true garments—not those of a dashing
rake but of a bungling, clumsy novice unable to succeed in the
seduction of a fifteen-year-old even with the assistance of an
experienced bawd, Mrs. Jewkes. Fielding's filling out of his
name was hardly necessary; Richardson had painted him a
booby in the original.

Pamela illustrates in the most extreme form a practice already objected to in Fielding's plays, marriage based on mercenary motives. Not even the warmest defender can deny that
Pamela is motivated by such principles and has different
standards for those of high and low rank. She endures from
Mr. B__, because of his wealth and position, what she would
never have suffered from a social equal. She is bargaining
with a buyer who can afford to go very high in the bidding.
While Mr. B__ is not motivated by mercenary considerations,
he is fully aware of the social chasm between himself and
Pamela, and his final decision to marry Pamela is no sounder
in principle than Pamela's. He is unable to enjoy the girl in
any other way, and enjoy her he will, even at the price of marriage.

The important thing in Pamela, as Samuel Johnson insisted,
is the sentiment; at Fielding's hands, Pamela no more escapes
exposure in her high sentiments than in her motives. One of
the most damaging strokes of the parody is the revelation of
the falseness of her protestations of modesty and maidenli-
ness. For an innocent she is too much preoccupied with con-
templation of her own beauty; with her inclination toward Mr.
B__, though not so ungovernable as to cause any reduction in
her price; and with Mr. B__'s lecherous intentions. Her first

question on recovering from her fainting fits after each of Mr.
B__'s attempts to rape her—Did he or didn't he?—clearly indicates this preoccupation, and, it should be added, her concern for the commodity which she hopes to sell in return for
marriage. Even after her engagement to Mr. B__ is settled,
she spends much of her time in analyzing her alternating fears
and anticipation of matrimony. Fielding points up this "porno-
graphic melodrama"[32] by allowing Shamela the uninhibited
indulgence of her desires with Parson Williams and by revealing her frustration when Booby fails to brush aside her fragile
defenses. (Henrietta Maria Honora Andrews upbraids her
daughter [Letters III, V] not for immorality but for her reck-
lessness with Williams, which it would be folly to repeat.
"Take care," she cautions, "to be well paid before-hand.")

    Fielding had only to allow Shamela to express her motiva-
tion in dealing with Booby, and the house built on Pamela's
virtue came tumbling down. Pamela is revealed

    [in] her vanity, her...sentimentality, her sanctimoni-
    ous parade of piety, her aggressive and self-conscious
    chastity, her secret pleasure in the temptations to which
    she prudently abstained from yielding; and dextrous man-
    oeuvering to secure the rewards of virtue both in this
    world and the next.[33]

The most devastating element of the parody is that Fielding
annihilates Pamela's morality by skillfully manipulating Richardson's own inventions—characters, scenes, and even dialogue are often reproduced almost identically. As effective
as Shamela is in exposing the shallowness of the ethical outlook of Pamela, it is, by the very limitations of parody, merely negative. The satirist is under no compulsion to provide a
substitute for what he destroys, but he is of course more effective when he does so. In his second attack on Pamela Fielding does present a positive alternative to the philosophy and
the characters under attack.

    Although Joseph Andrews (1742), the greatest of all the
anti-Pamelas, opens as though it is a parody, it is only inci-

dentally a burlesque and has from the start a design and life
of its own independent of <u>Pamela</u>. The references, as Battestin shows, are satirically allusive rather than imitative.[34]
The novel is much more than a story of courtship and marriage, just as it is more than a parody. It records the progress of naive virtue through an evil world. Joseph, the symbol of chastity, and Adams, of charity, are the standard bear-
ers "of a primitive Christianity, unadulterated by the compro-
mises with which the world has tempered its idealism."[35]
Among their experiences Joseph's frequently fall within the
area of the present study.

The point of departure in <u>Joseph Andrews</u>, as in <u>Pamela</u>,
is a moral one—the attempt on virtue, with the attack reversed.
In <u>Pamela</u> virtue, though not ordinarily to be defined as the
single quality of chastity, is clearly equated with chastity, as
Shamela's lack of "vartue" had been equated with her lack of
chastity. Thus from the very start in <u>Joseph Andrews</u>, Fielding challenges the limitation of the term by raising the question of male chastity, a virtue likely to be viewed in his day as
improbable and unnecessary. Lady Booby's tirade is an adequate expression of the common opinion:

> Did ever mortal hear of a man's virtue! Did ever the
> greatest, or the gravest man pretend to any of this kind!
> Will magistrates who punish Lewdness, or parsons who
> preach against it, make any scruple of committing it
> (I, 8)?

Lady Booby's contempt echoes down through the years in
varying tones of disbelief, amusement, and dissatisfaction as
the critics struggle with the "problem" of Joseph's chastity.
Dobson in 1883, supporting the idea that Fielding stumbled into
the larger theme of the book and abandoned the original idea of
merely another parody, writes that Fielding "must have been
secretly conscious that the 'Pamela' characteristics of his
hero were artistically irreconcilable with the personal brav-
ery and cudgel-playing attributes with which he had endowed
him."

The efforts of present-day critics to justify Joseph's virtue

lend ironic support to Shamela's Parson Williams in his text
"Be not righteous over-much." Kreissman labels Joseph a
prig in the opening episodes.

> He is far more chaste than his contemporaries would
> believe necessary or even possible. His virtue is not
> that of his fellows, but an extreme exaggeration of his
> own vanity. This exaggeration is an ugliness which
> clothes itself in the beauty of virtue. [37]

Kreissman, however, acquits Joseph of the charge of affectation: soon it is evident that his virtue is inspired by love for
the beautiful Fanny Goodwill. The inevitable deduction from
Kreissman's reasoning is that chastity based on the love of
virtue for its own sake is ridiculous (in Fielding's sense of
the term) but chastity based on love of a woman is pardonable.
Such a conclusion is unsatisfactory. The charge of vanity
against Joseph does not agree with Fielding's own definition
set forth in the introduction of the novel. Affectation, which
is the true source of the ridiculous, springs from vanity or
hypocrisy. Vanity results from the attempt to affect a given
virtue to a degree greater than one possesses it, in order to
win applause; hypocrisy, from the attempt to be thought the
reverse of what one is, in order to avoid censure. On neither
charge is Joseph guilty; his chastity is a real virtue and his
persistence in it is not designed to win applause. If this were
not the case, Fielding's whole design of contrasting Joseph and
Pamela would fall apart, for Joseph would be a Pamela of the
male sex.

Maurice Johnson attributes the humor of the temptation of
Joseph not to any inherent humor in male chastity but rather
to the comic setting. "When the reader laughs, it is because
of Lady Booby's miscalculation...and then because her bid
for Joseph is echoed by Mrs. Slipslop's cruder, below-stairs
onslaught."[38] Actually humor exists on more than one level in
this episode, as in the others involving Joseph's temptations.
Fielding is making use in this instance, as he does in every
satiric situation, of the existence of certain moral standards

and more or less fixed codes of social behavior generally accepted by his audience. By the test of the standards of the time, Lady Booby is ridiculous to her contemporaries on the most obvious level, as a superannuated coquette who cloaks her overtures to a much younger man in the language of virtue. She is further ridiculous because she violates the accepted code when she bemeans herself to make advances to an inferior. Joseph's rebuff is the last stroke in the portrait of hypocrisy and affectation. Her subsequent behavior, the chase into the country after Joseph and eventual acceptance of a captain of the dragoons, serves to further expose and cheapen her. Lady Booby and Mrs. Slipslop are illustrations of affectation as Fielding defines it and are proper objects of ridicule; Joseph is not. He is of course laughable in his inability to extricate himself with finesse from a situation which requires a sophistication he does not possess. The laughter which Joseph inspires is of a different sort from that directed at Lady Booby and Mrs. Slipslop.

The furore over Joseph's chastity easily obscures the fact that several levels of satiric humor may exist, and usually do, in a single situation. A sophisticated reader expecting a set of standards comparable to Pamela's and Lady Booby's, finds a strangely different set in Joseph. Joseph cannot cope with his world; hence he is funny. He is laughable, though not contemptible, because he is not artfully affected in an artfully affected society. His naive goodness contrasts throughout the novel with Pamela's sophistication, that is, her artful simplicity. Her seeming innocence is calculated; his innocence is real. Moreover, the reader is aware that Joseph's values are those to which society at least pays lip service. The predicament of one who attempts to practice the commandment of chastity, which all parrot, contributes to the satire. These overt and implied levels of satire exist throughout Joseph Andrews, and of course in all of Fielding's work.

Battestin relates Joseph's chastity to the author's reputation and the more human heroes to come, Tom Jones and Captain Booth, notwithstanding the illogicalness of confusing Fielding with his fictional characters and of using the later characters as a standard for judging the earlier ones.

> It would, of course, be scarcely conceivable that the au-
> thor of <u>Tom Jones</u> should undertake his first novel as a
> straight-faced defense of male chastity, in any narrow
> sense of the term. This was the age of the "double stan-
> dard"...and Fielding himself...seems to have been
> more than a little given in his youth to amorous conver-
> sation with the ladies.[39]

Although Joseph's virtue is, to Battestin, a "little hard to
bear," he does not underestimate the importance of male chastity in Fielding's morality, for, as he points out, the later
novels deal forcefully with the ills resulting from incontinence.[40]

The difficulty in treating Joseph as a "realistic" young man
is that his role as a symbol of chastity, presented as it is in a
comic manner, is hard to reconcile with the interpretation of
him as an average man, which he was never intended by Fielding to represent. The critics agree that Joseph is an increasingly attractive and forceful figure as the book progresses,
i. e. after his relationship to Fanny is introduced in Book II,
Chapter 12. He is too realistic—strong, impetuous in his love
for Fanny, sensible in his dealings with Adams—to be the
chaste Joseph of the earlier chapters. The fact that Joseph is
a comic character complicates analysis of him as a positive,
serious figure. Nevertheless, Fielding does present behind
the masks of satire certain implied alternatives to the objects
under attack. Joseph is treated on serious levels of meaning
as well as comic; and he achieves a dignity and a stature and
an elevation of personality far beyond the original limitations
of the initial burlesque mood.[41]

In dealing with Joseph, one inevitably returns to the original
moral issue: is chastity possible in a young man of normal
capacities? Fielding portrays him as such. For the satiric
purposes of the novel Joseph <u>must</u> be chaste if he is to fulfill
Fielding's conception of a contrast to Pamela. Such an argument as the basis of his virtue on the serious level, however,

is no more satisfactory than the justification of Squire Allworthy's actions in <u>Tom Jones</u> as the result of the necessities of plot manipulation. Fielding's affirmative answer should and does have a more valid basis than the mechanics of plot. Joseph's chastity is the triumph of reason over the passions, not merely the dominance of one passion (love) over another (lust), as would be the case if only the love of Fanny restrains him from succumbing to his would-be seducers. It is necessary that he be a young man of warm instincts, as contrasted with Pamela's calculated control of her emotions. Certainly Joseph's virtue would not merit the name if the temptation is not real.

The first assault on Joseph corresponds to Mr. B__'s attack on Pamela. Lady Booby's suggestion that Joseph may make his fortune by his person is a lure which does not dazzle him, as his sister was dazzled by such a prospect; but he confesses to Pamela in his second letter, "I am glad she turned me out of the chamber as she did: for I had once almost forgotten every word [concerning chastity] Parson Adams had ever said to me" (I, 10).

The second assault is made by that "hungry tigress" Mrs. Slipslop. It is not difficult to conclude, in view of her "charms," that Joseph had less trouble resisting his own impulses than the "violent amorous hands" of Slipslop. He is literally saved by the bell which Lady Booby rings for her maid.

Betty, the chambermaid whose "constitution was composed of those warm ingredients," is the next to attempt Joseph's seduction. On this occasion he is obliged to use some violence to shut Betty out of the room, though he does so "contrary to his inclination." Battestin protests that this expulsion is continence carried to a ludicrous extreme.[42] Here again it should be noted that the satire exists on at least two levels. Joseph's discomfiture is laughable, but the scene also recalls the excessive ado in Mr. B__'s attempts to seduce a Pamela when there are so many willing Bettys in the world. Even the social status of Betty and Pamela is about the same. This intention seems unmistakable, for Fielding concludes the expulsion of Betty with his own interruption, tongue in cheek:

> How ought a man to rejoice that his chastity is always in
> his own power; that if he hath sufficient strength of mind,
> he hath always a competent strength of body to defend
> himself, and cannot, like a poor weak woman, be rav-
> ished against his will (I, 18)!

Pamela, of course, was the "poor weak woman" who could
have escaped Mr. B__'s efforts, had she really desired escape.

Joseph's resistance to the attempts of his pursuers is not
the result of indifference to feminine charms other than Fanny's but rather to his "sufficient strength of mind." By contrast, it is hard to imagine Pamela suffering the torments of
desire for Mr. B__; she is admittedly in some danger of being
raped but not of being swept away in a moment of her own ungovernable passion. Her "virtue" is under control; she is
able to use Mr. B__'s passion to her own purpose. Joseph's
strength of mind to resist his pursuers is based on the teaching ("Chastity is as great a virtue in man as in woman.") and
the example of Parson Adams (who "never knew any more than
his wife")—and the letters of Pamela. The facetious reminder
of Pamela's letters once more glaringly exposes the sham
morality expressed in those documents and their lack of value
in teaching real morality, contrary to Richardson's avowed
purpose. Joseph's is a positive virtue, proven in the test by
his reliance on "good advice and good examples" and on his
own reasoning ability. He is fortified in the struggle by his
honest love for a good woman.

It is an interesting inconsistency of the explanations of, or
apologies for, Joseph's chastity that no critic takes exception
to the perfect chastity of Parson Adams as being artistically
irreconcilable or inconceivable coming from the pen of Fielding. On the contrary, Adams has always been acknowledged
as Fielding's masterpeice of characterization, largely on the
grounds of his marvelous realism. He is the possessor of all
the masculine attributes which Dobson found artistically irreconcilable in Joseph; yet he has been chaste before marriage and faithful after marriage and, by his wife's testimony,

is a loving husband. It is his example which Joseph emu[
Whether Joseph is as credible as an average young ma[
Tom Jones or a Captain Booth or a young Henry Fielding, is
not the question; nor does the novel concern itself with whether there are many Josephs in the world. The reader clearly
sees that although Josephs are rare, Pamelas are not. For
Fielding's purpose, Joseph is a perfectly chaste young man,
virtuous for the love of virtue. Perhaps Fielding's real triumph in the creation of Joseph is that he succeeded in fashion-
ing an ideally good hero who remains human enough to trouble
the scholars to reconcile his perfection with his humanity.
Once exposed to the vanities of the world, Joseph matures sufficiently to assess the world competently enough and to see
people for what they are. He consciously rejects what is false,
particularly in relation to marriage (infra, p. 58), and it is often Joseph who leads Adams. One is left at the end of the novel
with the impression that Joseph is no longer the victim of quix-
otic delusions from which Adams seems unlikely ever to be
freed, though it should be added that Adams, like Quixote, has
a fundamental rightness on his side many times when he is
made ridiculous in the wicked practical world. Joseph is not
only a rejector of Potiphar's wife but is a Sancho Panza, practical as Adams–Quixote is wild, by worldly standards.

Not only does Joseph's real virtue remind one constantly of
the inadequacies of Pamela's principles, but the love-making
of Joseph and Fanny focuses the light of truth on the hypocrisy
of the Pamela-Mr. B__ affair. The mutual physical attraction
of Joseph and Fanny is emphasized throughout the novel; their
affection, dating from childhood, grew to such a degree that
Parson Adams "had with much ado prevented them from marrying." During a year's separation their love is nurtured only
by "mutual confidence in each other's fidelity" (I, 11). They
cannot communicate by letter for Fanny does not read or write,
and would not be prevailed upon "to transmit the delicacies of
her tender and chaste passion by the hands of an amanuensis"
(I, 11). This is, of course, a pointed reminder of Pamela's
facile pen and her willingness to have the history of her vic-
tory over Mr. B__ published for all the world to read.

Fanny is a more subtle contrast to Pamela than is Joseph. The method in the central, and greater, portion of the novel is altogether allusive, with no mention of Pamela; however, reminders are plentiful. Fanny and Pamela are both servant girls. Fanny, unlike Pamela, has not been trained above her station, nor does she aspire to raise herself by marriage. That she might have done so if she had pursued her advantage, as Pamela did, is at least implied in the offers of the unnamed squire (III, 12) and Beau Didapper (IV, 11) to keep her. She is subjected to an attempted abduction (III, 9-12) which recalls Pamela's experience. The sharpest contrast is between Fanny's open declaration of love for Joseph, with the acknowledgement of its physical side; and Pamela's deviousness and concealed preoccupation with Mr. B_'s lechery. [43] Fanny is the first of Fielding's chaste but "healthy" novel heroines who do not play coyly with the sentiment of love, more outstanding examples of which are Sophia and Amelia. Pamela's sanctimonious comment when it appears that Joseph and Fanny are brother and sister ("She said if he loved Fanny as he ought, with a pure affection, he had no reason to lament being related to her.") "synthesized all the sham and hypocritical pretense of Pamela's 'pure affection' as opposed to Fanny's brand, which never for an instant denies the hope of marriage." [44]

Although physical attraction is an important factor in Joseph and Fanny's love, they base their marriage on the firmer ground of merit. Booby, at the insistence of Pamela, tries to educate Joseph to his newly elevated social station and advises him to abandon Fanny. Booby assumes, in perfect conformity with the character of Mr. B_, that physical beauty is the only source of her attraction for Joseph and ironically assures Joseph that "beauty alone is a poor ingredient, and will make but an uncomfortable marriage" (the chief basis for his own marriage). Joseph answers that beauty is Fanny's least possession; he knows of no virtue she is not possessed of. Booby points out the difference between himself and Joseph: "My fortune enabled me to please myself; and it would have been as overgrown a folly in me to have omitted it as in you to do it." Joseph replies that it is also his fortune to please himself; while he has health he will support himself and Fanny in their own station, regardless of the opinion of the Boobys or of his own parents. Moreover, Joseph argues that Fanny is Pamela's equal. Pamela's answer, "She was my equal," exposes her snobbery in its ultimate form. If there was, after Shamela, anything of Pamela's morality left to demolish, Fielding destroys it in this scene. Shamela had transformed Pamela into an "artful and disreputable hussy"; Joseph Andrews presents her as "an eminently respectable but insufferable prig."[45]

Not all the pleas of class distinction, any more than the temptation of other women, can dissuade Joseph from his steadfast loyalty to Fanny. Joseph proposes to fetch a license and marry Fanny without further delay. The ceremony is deferred again, however, at the insistence of Parson Adams, who is determined to observe church forms rather than civil. Adams no doubt would have decried the abuses of civil law which permitted fraudulent marriage as well as marriages, though not illegal, based on greed, lust and numerous other unworthy motives against which the good parson inveighed. (See Appendix A.) Moreover, as a clergyman, he would have opposed a procedure which diminished the role of the church in encouraging the ideal of marriage as a spiritual as well as physical relationship. He cautions Joseph against hastily entering marriage as an indulgence of carnal appetites and thus finds opportunity for a sermon against all unrestrained passions. "All passions are criminal in their excess, even love itself"; this text is immediately forgotten by Adams when he is told that his favorite son has drowned. A tempest of emotion entirely overcomes him. With the discovery that the child has suffered only a dunking, Adams' joy is followed by the resumption of his sermon: "No, Joseph, do not give too much way to thy passions." To Joseph's retort that he does not practice what he preaches, Adams scolds the youth and warns him to love his wife with moderation and discretion. Mrs. Adams overhears this last bit of advice and undoes all the parson's efforts by insisting that the parson himself has been a "loving and cherishing husband"; and she in turn advises Joseph to "be as good a husband as you are able, and love your wife with all your body and soul, too," advice more to Joseph's—and Fielding's—liking (IV, 8).

When the marriage is at last performed, it is a ceremony gratifying all the conditions which for Fielding represented "a state of bliss scarce ever equalled." The married pair share a love that is a reasonable combination of physical attraction and innate worth. Their unraveled parentage achieves for them a satisfactory level of gentility and financial security. Even the ceremony itself is in accord with established form blessed by the church.

In addition to the example of love, constancy, and mutual trust provided by Joseph and Fanny themselves, in several digressions Fielding reinforces his stand that these are the only true bases for marriage. The digression on Mr. Wilson, variously denounced as better omitted[46] and defended as "the philosophic, as well as the structural, center of the book,"[47] is an example of Fielding's use of minor episodes to reinforce the major theme of a novel. If the novel is viewed in the larger scheme as Joseph and Adams' pilgrimage through the vanities of this world, the Wilson episode is then an economical method of exposing Adams to the ills of the city without taking Adams himself to London. Joseph's exposure to that city, painted as detrimental even in its brevity, had ended abruptly with Lady Booby's advances and his subsequent dismissal. The relation of Mr. Wilson's progress through every vice of the city, ending with his rescue and regeneration through the love and generosity of his wife-to-be, provides a sermon on vanity, the general theme of the novel as a whole.

Wilson's education in matters of sex offers a testimonial to the consequences of indulgence in sexual promiscuity, not only those befalling him, but also the sad degeneration of one young woman who sinks from being his kept mistress to prostitution and finally death in Newgate. In praise of his wife, Wilson paints the ideal which Fielding elaborated in later novels: he calls Mrs. Wilson "a notable housewife," not learned "above the care of her family," and the instructress of her daughters in the arts of housewifery. The Wilsons' happy retirement,

declares Parson Adams, must be the "manner in which the
people had lived in the Golden Age" (III, 4). And it is to this
same manner that Joseph and Fanny will retire to their Eden-
retreat in the country to live out their happy lives, inheritors
of the Wilsons in every sense.

The tale of Leonora is no more a mere casual interlude in
the picaresque than is Mr. Wilson's story. Both tales provide
variations on the main themes of the book: charity, romance,
and love. The digression reiterates the ills of bad education
of women and marriage based on mercenary motives. Dazzled
by Bellarmine's show of finery and French manners, Leonora
jilts her faithful lover, only to discover that Bellarmine's sole
interest in her was the dowry he expected. Disappointed in
this, he leaves Leonora to a fate she deserved. Arnold Kettle
finds in the episode more than a crude homily on the consequences of Leonora's conduct; it allows Fielding to comment
once again on the inadequacy of conception of such a story,
which has "all the crudities, moral and technical (including
the idiotic letters got by heart) of a Pamela.... Leonora un-
derlines the incipient immorality of Pamela's attitude to
love."[48]

Lady Booby also provides a commentary, not a bright one,
on fashionable marriage. She is the strongest character link
between Fielding the dramatist and Fielding the novelist. She
might have stepped from the Restoration comedy, so perfect a
stereotype of the woman of fashion is she. She has had a town
education, scorns her country neighbors, and prefers the
frivolous gaieties of the city to the sober life of the country.
Her devotion to her husband dates from the hour of his death;
the first six days of her mourning she spends with no consolation except three friends and Mrs. Slipslop, just enough to
make a party at cards. Joseph describes the marriage to
Pamela: "They quarreled almost every day of their lives... and
I have heard her ladyship wish his honour dead above a thousand times" (I, 6). The match has all the earmarks of a marriage of convenience with little love or respect on either side.

Through these variations on the theme, as well as the central story, Fielding goes beyond the merely destructive de-

vices of Shamela to provide in Joseph Andrews an ethical alternative: the principle of marriage based on love and merit
and characterized by mutual trust. It offers as partners in
happy marriage lovers who acknowledge the physical as well
as spiritual nature of love and marriage. The joys of family
life are founded on harmony between husband and wife, both of
whom are to be examples as well as instructors to their children. The father is of course the dominant figure; the ideal
wife's chief concern is the pleasure of her husband and the
care of her home and children. The environment most condu-
cive to such an existence is the country. Because of the comic mode, the alternative is often implied rather than stated;
not all of these conditions are actually seen in Joseph and Fanny's marriage, as the novel ends with the ceremony. The alternative is nonetheless clear. Moreover, Fielding assures us
that the desired conditions, already sketched briefly in the
Wilsons' idyllic union, were fulfilled in due course for the
true lovers.

Of Fielding's four greatest works, Jonathan Wild offers the
least material significant to the marriage debate. This is
true not only because the book is primarily a political satire
and thus places less emphasis on the subject of marriage than
the other novels, but also because the portrayal of marriage
in this masterpiece of sustained irony hearkens back to the
conventional attitudes and techniques of the plays, lending at
least some support to the theory that Jonathan Wild was begun
earlier than Joseph Andrews. It does provide, even though on
a level subordinate to the political satire, a vivid criticism of
fashionable marriage.

Most critics agree that Jonathan Wild, published as part of
the Miscellanies of 1743, was completed or extensively rewrit-
ten in 1742, though possibly begun earlier as another blow in
the literary war against Robert Walpole.[49] Fielding's dramatic contributions to this cause in large measure precipitated
the Licensing Act of 1737, which ended his career in the theatre. Such plays as Grub Street Opera, Pasquin, and The Historical Register for 1736 had directed caustic hits against

Walpole as well as against corruption in government generally. The edition of <u>Jonathan Wild</u> revised by Fielding in 1754,
the one usually reprinted, eliminated or disguised numerous
passages aimed at Walpole, since his fall was an accomplished
fact in 1742.[50] The changes in this edition are consistently
toward generalization.

Fielding says of his purpose that he did not intend in the
character of his hero

> to represent human nature in general.... But without
> considering Newgate as no other than human nature with
> its mask off...we may be excused for suspecting, that
> the splendid palaces of the great are often no more than
> Newgate with the mask on.[51]

Having established the Newgate point of view, Fielding follows
the tradition of contemporary literature, already popularized
in John Gay's <u>The Beggar's Opera</u> and <u>Polly</u> and in his own
<u>Grub Street Opera</u>, in satirizing the manners and morals of
fashionable society by drawing an analogy with low life.[52] The
social satire is sharpest in the narration of the courtship and
marriage of Jonathan Wild and Laetitia Snap. The parody of
the conventions of fashionable marriage reduces to absurdity
the kind of high-life alliance which was based on nothing but
interest.

The conventional elements of courtship are ironically presented in Jonathan's distinguished ancestry,[53] education, and
prestige and in Laetitia's scrupulous attention to her reputation, while she indulges in numerous intrigues. The fathers
arrange the marriage with great solemnity, particularly in
negotiating the dowry of the bride (seventeen pounds and nine
shillings in money and goods) and the estate of Jonathan (a
third share in a chair). Jonathan eagerly presses the match
because of his love for the "chaste" Laetitia, who indeed with-
holds her favors from almost no one except him. His love is
an excessive desire to enjoy her person, which is the only understanding he has of "what simple people call love." His passion is of the honorable breed: he will go to any length, even

marriage, to satisfy it. Laetitia's consent to the match is given in an indifferent spirit of obedience to her father's desire for a profitable alliance and with assurance that marriage will not interfere with a lady's freedom. The tranquil felicity usually implied by the author who rings down his curtain with the marriage ceremony is not, however, says Fielding, the lot of Jonathan and Laetitia.

Jonathan was not, before or after marriage, of that "low, snivelling breed of mortals who...tie themselves to a woman's apron-strings; in a word, who are tainted with that mean, base, low vice, or virtue as it is called, of constancy" (I, 3). Having satisfied his passion, Jonathan loathed and detested what he had before ardently desired. Emphasis upon the brevity of that passion which men call "love," more accurately termed "hunger," which is based on appetite alone, recurs frequently in Fielding's novels, e.g., Tom Jones, VI, 1; Booth's relations with Miss Matthews, Amelia; and of course numerous other instances to be expected of the libertines like the unnamed rich peer and James in Amelia. Laetitia was no happier in the marriage than her husband but for a somewhat different reason: her dissatisfaction stemmed from her discovery that one man is not as good as ten (II, 7). Consequently, the two agree at the end of a fortnight to live civilly together, that is, not as man and wife.

The truce scene (II, 8), evidence of the influence of Fielding's dramatic career on his novel writing, is presented in dramatic form. There is even an echo of the dialogue of An Old Man Taught Wisdom, when Blister tells Lucy that the actual marriage of a fashionable couple need last no more than a fortnight, after which each is free to pursue his own pleasure. In the parley over conditions of the truce, Laetitia and Jonathan lay down terms familiar in the proviso scenes of such Restoration plays as Congreve's The Way of the World (IV, 1).[54]

Laet.   You agree I shall converse with whomsoever I please?

Jon.   Without control: And I have the same liberty?

Laet.   When I interfere may every curse you wish
        attend me!
Jon.   Let us now take a farewell kiss, and may I
        be hanged if it is not the sweetest you ever
        gave me (III, viii).

In spite of the truce, so great was the hatred of the Wilds for
each other that they "never could bear to see the least com-
posure in one another's countenance without attempting to ruf-
fle it." With many opportunities for executing this malice,
they seldom passed one easy or quiet day together (III, 9).

The climax of the parody of fashionable marriage occurs in
a mock-discovery scene. Fielding uses one of his favorite devices, the mock-epic simile, in this case a very vulgar one,
to describe Wild's rage and the uproar which follows the revelation of injury done to his honor by Laetitia and his friend
Fireblood. Wild and Fireblood argue at length the fine points
of honor; the debate is followed by a duel, in this case, fisti-
cuffs. When the fight is interrupted by their prison mates, the
two promise satisfaction if "they outlived the ensuing sessions
and escaped the tree" (IV, 10).

The ironic intent of the portrayal of the Wilds' marriage is
heightened by the introduction of the Heartfrees, the "silly
people" who serve throughout the novel as a foil to the Wilds,
the great man and the woman of spirit. The Heartfrees belong
to "the pitiful order of mortals" called good-natured and are
thus the object of contempt. They of course achieve the tranquility beyond the attainment, and comprehension as well, of
the Wilds. Thomas Heartfree, "a silly fellow" exhibiting such
weaknesses of mind as generosity, good-nature, and friendli-
ness, married for love a very agreeable woman, that is, one
who was "mean-spirited, poor, domestic, and low bred" (II,
1). Mrs. Heartfree, unlike the fashionable Laetitia, confined
herself

mostly to the care of her family, placed her happiness
in her husband and her children, followed no expensive
fashions or diversions, indeed rarely went abroad, unless to return the visits of a few plain neighbors, and

twice a year afforded herself, in company with her husband, the diversion of a play, where she never sat in a higher place than the pit ((II, 1).

The difference between the bad wife and the good one is highlighted by their behavior during the adversities of the husbands. Laetitia visits Jonathan after his imprisonment only because she has also been arrested for picking pockets, and she uses the occasion to berate him for the disgrace he has brought on her, chiefly through ignoring her wifely advice. She concludes her tirade with the declaration that it almost makes amends for being hanged herself to have the pleasure of seeing him hanged too. This "fond couple" parts with Jonathan flinging Laetitia out of the room, "but not before she had with her nails left a bloody memorial on his cheek" (IV, 2). During a second visit Laetitia plagued, tormented, and upbraided him so cruelly that he forbade the keeper to admit her again. She did, however, return on the eve of Jonathan's execution, but the reunion, which promised to be a tender one, ended with denunciations and violence. Jonathan interrupted her recapitulation of his faults in an exact order, seized her by the hair, and kicked her from the room.

Mrs. Heartfree, on the other hand, quickly recovers from her first "tears and lamentations" over the news of her husband's arrest and sets about with great practicality to procure his liberty. When she is unsuccessful, she goes to the prison to comfort him with her presence. Each is entirely concerned with the welfare of the other. Mr. Heartfree laments the distress his imprisonment will bring to his wife and children; she attempts to paint their difficulties as less than they are and to raise his hopes for release. Moreover, she cautions him against endangering his health by despair, for "no state of life could appear unhappy to her with him, unless his own sorrow made it so. (Cf. Amelia, IV, 3: "I can level my mind with any state...you have a wife who will think herself happy with you, and endeavor to make you so, in any situation." Also IV, 9: Amelia "knew no happiness out of his company.") Thus, adds Fielding, did this weak poor-spirited woman attempt to relieve her husband's pains, which it would have rather become her to aggravate, by not only painting out his misery in the liveliest colours imaginable, but by upbraiding him and by lamenting her own hard fate in being obliged to share his sufferings (II, 7).

Although the contrast between a bad marriage and a good one is in itself sufficient to warrant an examination of Jonathan Wild, its greatest significance for this study is the similarity between Mrs. Heartfree and Amelia. It is one of the interesting curiosities of literary fate that the very language with which Fielding ironically described Mrs. Heartfree—"low," "mean-spirited," and "domestic"—reverberates in the denunciations which greeted Amelia. Fielding enumerates the charges in the famous defense of his "favorite child" before the Court of Censorial Enquiry of The Covent-Garden Journal: Amelia has been condemned, he says, as "a low Character," a "Milksop"; she shows "no Manner of Spirit unless in supporting Afflictions"; not abusing her husband was "contemptible meanness."[55] In fact, the similarity of the charges brought ironically by Fielding against Mrs. Heartfree and seriously against Amelia by contemporary critics, accustomed to the tradition of the fashionable woman and of Pamelas aspiring to high life, results from the basic identity of the characters and the difficulties they face. Mrs. Heartfree is of course scarcely developed, but the pattern is the same.

Like Amelia, Mrs. Heartfree is a paragon of wifely and maternal virtues. Heartfree praises her as the best of women: "she had every perfection, both of mind and body." She finds her whole pleasure in her husband and children, and, like Amelia, enjoys domestic activities more than fashionable pastimes.

Mrs. Heartfree's greatest test is of her faithfulness to her marriage vows. Most of the trials occur in the course of the digressive tale (IV, 7-12) which relates Mrs. Heartfree's marvelous adventures after her escape from Wild. The most widely held theory is that the digression was intended as a

parody of the extravagant travel tales current.[56] Irwin points
out the possibility that in addition to satirizing the travel-tales,
Fielding may have intended Mrs. Heartfree's indefatigable defense of her virtue as yet another thrust at Pamela's steadfast
resistance and at numerous extravagant seduction accounts in
popular romances.[57] This interpolated tale again illustrates
Fielding's ability, already noted in the Wilson and Leonora
digressions in Joseph Andrews, to accomplish several satiric
purposes at once. Whichever satiric thread one wishes to emphasize, it must be admitted that Mrs. Heartfree is portrayed
as a woman of considerably more presence of mind and spirit
than the typical heroine of the seduction romances or the travel stories. In preserving her virtue and spurning a parade of
amorous suitors who constantly besiege her, not once does she
resort to swooning, the favorite escape of these heroines.

The first assault is made by Wild, who

conceived that passion... which gentlemen of this our age
agreed to call LOVE, and which is indeed not other than
that kind of affection... a lusty divine is apt to conceive
for the well-drest sirloin... which the well-edified squire
in gratitude sets before him, and which, so violent is his
love, he devours in imagination the moment he sees it
(II, 8).

Wild, like most of the others who pursue Mrs. Heartfree,
clothes his hungry passion under the guise of friendship for
the husband and the desire to protect the defenseless woman.
Mrs. Heartfree in turn repulses Wild, the French captain, the
brutish English captain, Count La Ruse, the hermit, the African chief, and the captain of the slave ship.

In all of these trials Mrs. Heartfree shows the self-reliance
and conviction characteristic in greater degree of Sophia and
Amelia. For instance, she defends herself against the English
captain by encouraging him to drink himself into a stupor so
that she can escape from his cabin. The most unusual of her
suitors is the African chief, who according to the custom of
his tribe, offers an immense gift in return for her consent to

accept him as a lover. When she refuses, he respects her wish, illustrating the superiority of his natural goodness and his primitive code over that of civilized men who ravish unwilling women. The chief bestows upon Mrs. Heartfree a rich jewel, symbolic of but less valuable than her chastity (IV, 11).

Mrs. Heartfree concludes the narrative of her adventures with the declaration that "Providence will sooner or later procure the felicity of the virtuous and innocent." Fielding nicely arranges for Providence to accommodate her faith. Mr. Heartfree is cleared of the false charges; the two are reunited and grow old in purest love and friendship. They enjoy the happiness of seeing the older daughter married to the faithful apprentice and having the younger daughter devote her life to the care of her parents. Such affection and amity reigned among the members of this family that it was called the "family of love." The joys of mutual family love receive only a little less emphasis in this novel than in Amelia, with many scenes depicting the children's devotion to their parents.

The similarities between Amelia and Mrs. Heartfree are numerous and clear; however, it must be added that Mrs. Heartfree never attains the interest and reality of Amelia. She is, in fact, hardly less colorless than her virtuous but gullible husband. The Heartfrees are little more than admirable shadows and that is all that is necessary for the subordinate role they play as foils for Laetitia and Jonathan, who are the vivid instance of all that is false in marriage. Allowing for the extravagances in presenting his case consistently in the ironic mode, Fielding clearly shows the results of the one marriage to be destructive; and of the other, that happiness which he conceived of as the greatest human beings can experience, mutual and chaste conjugal love.

It is obvious that in both Joseph Andrews and Jonathan Wild, Fielding is dealing with courtship and marriage incidental to his larger purpose, a satire on vanities and a satire on false greatness. Nevertheless, he subjects the disparity between the ideal and the reality of marriage to some pointed analysis even in these subordinated treatments of the topic. He is clearly formulating the values he expresses with increasing

force in Tom Jones and with finality in Amelia. In these later
novels the problems of courtship and marriage are the plot
material of primary concern. Joseph Andrews bears somewhat the same relation to Tom Jones as Jonathan Wild to
Amelia, in that the former are concerned chiefly with the
problems of courtship and the latter with the problems of marriage. An examination of the later novels will reveal Fielding's final views on the subject.

Chapter 4

MARRIAGE IN THE LATER NOVELS:
TOM JONES

In the early novels, Fielding's central interest is, as we have seen, not in the portrayal of courtship and marriage, so that what he has to say about these subjects is sometimes implicitly rather than explicitly set forth, sometimes incidentally introduced. With the later novels we come to Fielding's full-fledged serious treatment, in Tom Jones (1749), of the problems of courtship and, in Amelia (1751), of marriage.

The requirements of the parody frame had imposed limitations in choice of characters and in at least the initial material of Joseph Andrews. This was not the case in Tom Jones. Fielding was free to present in the central figure as well as in the peripheral ones a totally realistic human being. The objection to Joseph that he is a figure out of romance, a kind of low-life St. George clad in the armor of chastity and slaying dragons of hypocrisy and vanity in a real enough world to win his servant-girl lady fair, cannot be made against Tom Jones. Not only is Tom's world real, but Fielding has created in Tom a hero who exemplifies the average natural man, as Joseph had the extraordinary man. Moreover, since the novel promises as its fare Human Nature (I, 1), Tom struggles against a greater variety of obstacles, both external and inner, than the earlier hero had faced. Joseph had to overcome only obstacles of an external nature; consequently he is a less complex character than Tom. Complexity here refers to the realism of the characters. Tom has nothing about him of parody, as Joseph has. The complexity of Fielding's art is certainly greater in Joseph. Like Joseph, Tom is tested; unlike Joseph, he fails. Although Tom wins his lady's love, unlike Joseph, he must overcome social opposition based on the inequality of his situ-

ation and Sophia's. He faces not only the obstacle of illegitimate birth, and presumably base to boot, but also a more formidable consideration, the lack of wealth. More important to
Fielding than these social and economic considerations is the
moral issue—Tom's ultimate success depends upon his learning prudence, a lesson Joseph is already master of when his
trials begin. For Fielding, prudence meant not only upright,
wise living but also the appearance of it. In addition to the
difficulties facing Tom, Sophia must make choices which are
also social, involving her choice of a lover beneath her in
rank; and moral, involving her disobedience of her father.
Thus, in Tom and Sophia, Fielding combines all the major social, economic, and moral motifs of the entire marriage question. Moreover, surrounding the central characters are a
number of relevant commentaries afforded by other marriages
which form a kind of tapestry effect against which Tom and
Sophia's story is woven.

From the outset of the novel Tom's position in society is
anomalous. This is nowhere more clearly evident than in the
variable treatment he receives in the Allworthy household
from everyone but the squire. Allworthy, consistently kind
and generous, rears the boy as the equal of Blifil. To the
others who enjoy the largesse of Allworthy, Tom is a pawn in
the game of currying the squire's favor or venting personal
grudges. Even Bridget is capricious in her behavior toward
her unacknowledged son, alternately showering him with affection or ignoring him, usually in direct relation to her desire
to turn any inkling of suspicion of maternity from herself and
later to annoy her husband, Captain Blifil (II, 7). In the world
at large Tom's situation is well summed up by an unnamed
landlady: so long as he is assumed to be a gentleman's son,
i.e., with a gentleman's resources, though he is a "bye-blow,"
he will be treated as a gentleman; "for many of these bye-
blows come to be great men" (VIII, 4). Among those to whom
a match between Tom and Sophia is a matter of concern, Tom's
birth is of no consequence until the subject of marriage arises.

Tom's illegitimacy troubles Western not at all. He loves
the boy best of his hunting companions; indeed, "everything

which the squire held most dear, to wit, his guns, dogs, and horses" (III, 10), is at the command of Tom. Even with the squire's daughter, Tom has free communication, but not of course as a suitor. Although the squire frequently calls Tom a bastard, he never states his objections to a marriage in terms of the youth's illegitimacy. Mrs. Western rails at Sophia for thinking of disgracing the family by allying herself to a bastard (VI, 5), but she gives ample evidence that her strongest objection to Tom is his lack of an inheritance. She espouses the cause of Blifil only until a wealthier prospect appears in Lord Fellamar. Her lectures to Sophia run constantly on one theme—worldly prudence consists in considering matrimony only as a means of making one's fortunes and advancing in the world. Matrimony to this female politician from London is "a fund in which prudent women deposit their fortune...in order to receive a larger interest for them than they could have elsewhere" (VIII, 3). This "prudent" view of matrimony is exactly that so often ridiculed by Fielding.

Fielding's own attitude concerning illegitimacy is expressed by Allworthy early in the novel. Fearing Allworthy's partiality to Tom over his own son (delivered, Fielding notes with irony, eight months after the nuptials), Captain Blifil never misses an opportunity to denounce on Biblical authority the keeping of the illegitimate child as a countenancing of sin. Such "children of nobody" should be brought up, he argues, to the lowest and vilest offices of the commonwealth. Allworthy rejects Blifil's arguments; for "however guilty the parents might be, the children were certainly innocent.... To represent the Almighty as avenging the sins of the guilty on the innocent was indecent, if not blasphemous" (II, 2).

Fielding might easily have provided a suitable legal father as a part of the unraveling of the marvelous plot, but his persistence in leaving Tom an illegitimate hero, which bewildered the apostle of respectability, Richardson, speaks as convincingly for Fielding's convictions as Allworthy's statement. However, Fielding allows Sophia the final say on her lover's base birth:

So brave, and yet so gentle; so witty, yet so inoffensive;
so humane, so civil, so genteel, so handsome! What
signifies his being base born, when compared with such
qualifications as these (VI, 5)?

Ian Watt regards birth as the determining factor in Fielding's plot, "almost the equivalent of money in Defoe or virtue
in Richardson." Money is "something good characters either
have or are given or momentarily lose; only bad characters
devote any effort to getting or to keeping it....[It] is a useful
plot device but it has no controlling significance."[58] The primary problem, he continues, is to bring about the marriage of
Sophia and Tom without subverting the social order, that is, to
reveal Tom's true status. Sherburn, on the other hand, sees
no moral purpose in Tom's birth, only a device for initiating
the indispensable plot mystery.[59] Both interpretations require
some qualification, as Watt overstates the significance of gentle birth as much as Sherburn understates it. Birth was unquestionably of great importance to Fielding. His social philosophy, as Sherburn points out, is based on the concept of a
stratified society in which the duty of all classes is to contribute to the good of the whole.[60] Fielding believed that every
man, whatever his place in the scale, had an obligation to meet
his individual moral responsibility to his group and to society.
His ideal benevolent man was characterized by "liberality of
spirits," which he says he had "scarce ever seen in men of
low birth and education" (IX, 1). This liberality of spirits,
benevolence, or good-nature, as he variously labeled it, is the
distinguishing quality of all of his admirable figures. It was
from the well-born as a class that such men should logically
be expected to come. Significantly, he makes Tom genteel, if
illegitimate. However, Fielding is fully aware that a rascal
could be well born. Birth is no guarantee of those qualities
which Fielding extolled and no bar to their existing in the man
of low station. The strongest statement for his belief in an inherent difference in men is the contrast between Tom and his
half-brother. Blifil is the epitome of hypocrisy and malice,
not only willing to cheat his brother of his inheritance, but ac-

tively conniving to get him hanged. Nor is Blifil an isolated case; one may call the roll of the well-born characters other than Allworthy and find the benevolent individual almost entirely missing: Squire Western, Lord Fellamar, Bridget, Mrs. Western, Lady Bellaston, Mrs. Fitzpatrick, to name only the most obvious. Some of these are not malevolent, only unconcerned; however, both groups are condemned by Fielding for failing to live up to the advantages of their birth and the responsibilities which their position entailed. Much of his sharpest satire, and this is even more evident in <u>Amelia</u>, is directed at those individuals who shirk their social responsibilities because of selfishness or indifference.

Moreover, Fielding emphasizes the fact that his own concept of the importance of benevolence does not prevail, by creating a fictional world which placed the greater valuation on money, not birth. Money thus seems more than merely a useful device in the plot; it looms as a great issue in <u>Tom Jones</u>, and as an even greater one in <u>Amelia</u>. Fielding never made money the basis of a happy marriage; but as Mrs. Miller laments, there is no happiness in marriage without a competency (XIII, 8). It is questionable whether Fielding had so casual a view of the importance of money as suggested by Watt's statement, since he struggled all his life against the hardships of inadequate income; but granting that he valued the man more, society, he plainly shows, values money first. One need not diminish the importance of gentle birth to recognize his understanding that lack of wealth is a more formidable problem, as the world goes, than low birth. He solves the two problems simultaneously in fiction, bestowing an inheritance on Tom through the revelation that he is well born, the same method he had used in <u>Joseph Andrews.</u> Tom's obstacles of base birth and lack of wealth, however, as the solution of them reveals, are of an external nature. The really significant business of the novel is the educating of Tom into prudence and the practice of the religious convictions which he professes. Thus the real obstacle to his marriage is a moral one. The external obstacles can be removed only after Tom has realized his follies and proven more than the mere resolution to reform his life. The same process is necessary in Amelia; Booth's conversion precedes the solution of the externally caused difficulties, which are basically financial.

The relative significance of Tom's two external problems is clear in the line of opposition taken by the squire. The idea of a marriage between Tom and Sophia had never entered his head, simply because he considered

> a parity of fortune and circumstances to be physically as necessary an ingredient in marriage, as difference of sexes, or any other essential: and had no more apprehension of his daughter's falling in love with a poor man, than with any animal of a different species (VI, 9).

The squire's own marriage was based on the only motive he understands, financial considerations. The fact that it was a match far from satisfactory to either party (infra pp. 91-92) was not sufficient to provide any enlightenment about a woman's right to choose her own husband. His threat to turn Sophia out of doors to beg, starve, and rot in the street, though exaggerated for comic effect, is not an idle one and is not considered by Sophia as such. Tom for a long time suppressed any show of his true feelings for Sophia because he knew her father to be "perfectly a man of the world in whatever regarded his fortune...he had often signified...the pleasure he proposed in seeing her married to one of the richest men in the county" (V, 3). Western's eagerness to promote a match between Tom and Sophia once Allworthy names the youth his heir underscores the fact that for the squire it is Tom's lack of an inheritance that bars any union with Sophia.

Allworthy, although he is the champion of marriage based on love, is also aware of the practical side of matrimony. Worldly prudence, he concedes, exacts some consideration of fortune which he does not condemn. "As the world is constituted, the demands of a married state, and the care of posterity, require some little regard to what we call circumstances" (I, 12).[61] Pleased as he is at the prospect of an advantageous match for Blifil, Allworthy nevertheless insists that the mar-

riage be based on mutual consent. He wishes to see the day
when the laws of the country will restrain parents from forc-
ing a woman into marriage contrary to her wishes and denounces the parents who act in this manner as "accessories to
all the guilt which their children afterward incur" (XVII, 3).
Allworthy's indignation toward Tom is colored by the inaccur-
acy of the manner in which his conquest of Sophia is reported;
it is the supposed treachery, unanswered by Tom, and not the
fact that the two have fallen in love, which offends him.

Sophia and Tom themselves accept the standards of the
world in which they live; it is never their intention to defy
convention. With the mutual acknowledgment of love comes the
recognition of its hopelessness. Sophia is innocently trapped
into revealing feelings which she assures her aunt she meant
to carry to her grave. Her flight from home is to escape marriage and not to pursue Tom, whatever her secret hopes. She
offers her pledge never to marry against her father's wishes
if he will in turn not force her to marry against her will. What
seems to be the futility of their love influences the behavior of
both Sophia and Tom, and it is against this background that she
reacts, particularly to Tom's indiscretions.

Just as Joseph's chastity had engaged the chief attention of
critics of the earlier hero, so Tom's lack of that quality has
been the heart of most analyses of the later hero. It is the
sexual issue which is crucial both in the moral scheme of the
novel and in the objections of its critics,[62] from the date of
the novel's first appearance to the present. Confused with the
issue of Tom's morals is the association, or misassociation,
of Fielding with Tom Jones and later with Billy Booth, as re-
flections of himself. This tradition, based on contemporary
but unsubstantiated gossip and malice and perpetuated by such
an influential later critic as Thackeray, shows no signs of an
impending demise. Tom can be considered a study of Fielding
"only in the sense that any fiction of a biographical cast in
which there is a prominent central figure of the same sex as
the author is pretty sure to be based largely on self-observa-
tion, probably in the main unconscious."[63] To identify Tom
or Booth with Fielding any further than this is detrimental to

sound analysis of the fictional figures.

The moral scheme is the important issue in Tom Jones, for obviously Fielding is a moralist and has for the better part of a century finally received his due as an upright man and an earnest worker for reform. However, his morality was not the kind understood by many of his contemporaries; hence such charges as Johnson's attack on those familiar histories whose wicked heroes were made so attractive that "we lose all abhorrence of their faults" (Rambler, March 31, 1750). Tom exemplifies in its most persuasive form such a hero of mixed character.

Tom has all the goodness, generosity, and honor in his temper to make him worthy of happiness. His good nature, or benevolence, is translated many times into actions for the good of others, as Fielding believed true benevolence must be and so illustrated it in his good men. Indeed, Tom's indiscretions are frequently the result of liberality of spirit, which is the inevitable manifestation of good nature. For Fielding, a man good by nature can imagine other people's feelings so directly that he has an impulse to act on them as if they were his own; and this impulse, the basis of genuinely unselfish actions, is the source of one's greatest pleasure as well. This sympathetic impulse unrestrained by prudence is the basis of Tom's trouble. Some bitter experiences are to be endured by the all-too-human Tom before he achieves moral adulthood and is fit for marriage to Sophia. In exposing Tom to temptations, Fielding emphasizes that he is "discovering [that is, revealing] the rocks on which innocence and goodness split," not recommending the means by which they will be undone (III, 7).

Attacks on Tom's chastity provide the opportunities for exercise of prudence and religious conviction, but, as Tom sadly confesses, he cannot long pretend to the gift of chastity (XIV, 4). Attacks is the accurate word to describe the testing of Tom; for he is as much the pursued as Joseph had been. There is a striking parallel between the aggressors; Joseph's warm-blooded Betty has her counterpart in Molly and Mrs. Waters, and Lady Bellaston is a hardened Lady Booby. Tom's defense

that he has not injured any innocent woman is justified. This
point receives particular emphasis in Tom's first experience,
with Molly Seagrim. Although greatly attracted to Molly, Tom
stayed away from her for three months because the thought of
debauching a young woman, especially the daughter of a friend,
appeared to him a heinous crime. Molly, less innocent and
less concerned for her virtue than Tom imagined, grew pro-
portionately forward as Tom grew backward. "In a word, she
soon triumphed over all virtuous resolutions of Jones." Molly
played the role of reluctant so well that Tom fancied himself
the conqueror (IV, 6). Mrs. Waters is no less the aggressor
than Molly. During their walk to the inn after her rescue,
Mrs. Waters uses every opportunity to expose her charms to
Tom. Once at the inn, the "fair conqueror" turns against him
the "whole artillery of love": glances, sighs, smiles, and finally the unmasking of "the royal battery, by carelessly letting
her handkerchief drop from her neck" (IX, 5).

Fielding's technique of presenting the guile of Molly in
broadly ironic form and the premeditated strategy of Mrs.
Waters in the boisterous style of the mock-heroic reconciles
the reader to Tom's slips. In addition to treating Tom as the
victim, Fielding surrounds the foregoing incidents with so
much farcical humor, especially the Upton episode, that the
reader is likely to laugh away the seriousness of the breach of
morality involved. In fact, Fielding indicates that the violated
commandment is customarily more honored in the breach than
in the observance. Squire Western, for example, makes no
objection to Tom on the score of his indulgences. When it is
apparent that Tom is the father of Molly's expected child, the
squire is highly amused at having smoked out Tom. He defends him—"Where's the mighty matter o' it?"—and dispar-
ages the idea that Allworthy will be offended or that Tom will
suffer in the opinion of the ladies. Contrary to the squire's
judgment, the only persons in whose opinion he does suffer for
these indiscretions are Allworthy and Sophia.

Allworthy admonishes Tom, as he had Jenny Jones early in
the novel, to repent of the sin of incontinence, "however light-
ly it may be treated by debauched persons," for it is a defi-

ance of Divine command and inevitably brings social consequences of shame and misery (I, 7). Sophia is disillusioned to
discover that Tom can declare his love for her and still engage
—or submit—in one amour after another. Fielding takes care
to provide ample extenuating circumstances on which Sophia's
and the reader's pardon can be based: the kind of person Tom
is, the aggressiveness of his seducers, and the seeming hopelessness of his situation. Moreover, Fielding supports Tom's
plea that his amours had little to do with real love. In the
prologue to Book VI Fielding contrasts the grosser instinct,
the desire of "satisfying a voracious appetite with a certain
quantity of human flesh," more properly called hunger, with
that love of a higher order, based on esteem and gratitude.
"Though the pleasures arising from such pure love may be
heightened and sweetened by the assistance of amorous desires, yet the former can subsist alone" (VI, 1).

It is this effort of Fielding to put every phenomenon, including sexual virtue and sexual vice, into a broad moral perspec-
tive that confused and angered many, for the results do not
always produce the kind of emphasis moralists like. [64] Fielding does not excuse Tom's failure to discipline those passions
of love arising from appetite; he does imply that those are
not the most serious shortcomings a man can be guilty of. It
is clear, nonetheless, that the progress of incontinence from
the first indulgence with Molly to thoughtless acceptance of
Mrs. Waters' favors and finally to the indignity of being Lady
Bellaston's kept lover is a degenerative process. Along with
Tom, in time the reader recognizes that it brings Tom to the
brink of destruction.

The affair with Lady Bellaston, initially accepted by Tom
as a challenge of gallantry, becomes the most heinous of his
offenses to generations of critics of both the author and his
hero. Baker points out the paradox of the critics, railing at
Tom's lapse as if he had gone on deliberately earning the
wages of sin, since Fielding, whose ethics were usually in advance of the times, was in this episode true to the prevailing
standards. [65] However, the justification that no code existed
in Tom's day against a man's accepting money from a woman

is unsatisfactory for a number of reasons. Even the extenuating circumstances which Fielding carefully elaborates—Tom is destitute of hope as well as resources—do not dispel the unpleasant effect of this affair. Fielding's method accounts for this stronger reaction and thus suggests a conscious intention. It is necessary that Tom recognize the direction he is traveling; the reader, who may have been tolerantly amused by the Molly and Jenny Waters episodes, likewise must recognize Tom's progress downward. Fielding therefore abandons the boisterous humor attending the earlier lapses; there is nothing of wholesome bawdy in the last involvement. For women guilty mainly of too-warm constitution, Fielding substitutes a woman who is as malicious as she is lustful. She is reminiscent of Mrs. Modern in that she arouses not laughter but loathing. Further, Tom's view of himself reveals this offense as more serious than his dalliance with Molly or Jenny. Tom is fully aware of the consideration upon which all of Lady Bellaston's gifts are conferred. With Molly and Jenny, the desire was spontaneous and mutual; toward Lady Bellaston Tom feels no attraction. He owes a debt and his conscience smarts at the obligation. Moreover, although Lady Bellaston is despicable, the deceit practiced by Tom to extricate himself from the affair does not raise him in our eyes.

During this affair Tom does reach the realization of the full consequences of his incontinence; and, as he tells Mrs. Miller, he has resolved to "quit a life of which... [he] was sensible of the wickedness as well as folly" (XVII, 5). There is yet another shock, however, before his chastisement is sufficient, the revelation that he has apparently committed incest.

Like the Bellaston affair, the suggestion of incest is a point of contention among critics. Its use by Fielding is not peculiar to this novel; Fanny and Joseph briefly believe themselves to be sister and brother. Even earlier than <u>Joseph Andrews</u>, Fielding had used it in the play <u>The Wedding Day</u>, in which the timely revelation of daughter-father relationship between the bride and groom prevents incest. Dudden finds the device disagreeable in <u>Tom Jones</u> but attempts to account for it on moral grounds.

Perhaps it was necessary that Tom should be reduced to
the uttermost depth of horror and despair, that he might
be brought to the full and true repentance of his errors,
but some may wish that this result had been achieved by
some less shocking means. [66]

A Times Literary Supplement writer agrees in viewing this
frightening of Tom as a particularly moral part of the book, in
fact the one thing which makes the book important, since it re-
minds Tom, and the reader, that actions have their consequences. [67] Murry objects that the morality of the novel does
not depend on this episode and declares that to "a more normal
sensibility [it] constitutes the one doubtful moment in the book
—the one moment at which we feel that Fielding may have
sounded a false note." [68] Empson suggests that the basic reason for the incest scare may be the philosophical cast of Fielding's mind: Fielding found it "curious that those who laugh at
ordinarily illicit sex take incest very seriously." [69] This interpretation, one might add, strains the functions of the philosophical mind! Empson agrees that the incident is part of
the change in Tom's attitude but it is not a decisive factor, for
his resolution to reform his life had already been made before
Partridge revealed to Tom that he had been "a-bed with his
own mother."

Tom's moral descent had in fact ended with the Bellaston
affair. His progress toward maturity is evident while he is
still involved with her. As early as that he leads young Night-
ingale to abandon false notions of honor and to fulfill his obligation to Nancy Miller (XIV, 7). The upward progress is further indicated by his refusal of the rich young widow's proposal (XV, 11), the rejection of Mrs. Fitzpatrick's advances
and her suggestion that he make love to Mrs. Western to get
to Sophia (XVI, 9), and finally the rejection of Mrs. Waters'
overtures in prison (XVII, 9). The idea that he has accident-
ally committed incest is a sufficiently terrible blow to confirm
his determination to repent and reform, but it is not the motivation. The argument for this moral purpose is valid enough
in theory, but it is difficult to dismiss the impression that the

supposed incest is chiefly a trick to heighten and prolong sus-
pense at the end of the novel. For one thing, the knowing
reader of Fielding is perhaps not so horrified as the commentators cited above suggest; he does not expect tragic horror
from Fielding—from Richardson, yes, but not from Fielding.
As Empson says, when the incest theme is introduced, the
action has reached the point when Tom must go right up or
right down.

Since it is right up to a reconciliation with Allworthy and
marriage that Tom moves, we may well consider the conclusions that Fielding wishes us to make about Tom. He has been
guilty of errors which Fielding on the one hand condemns as a
disobedience to a Christian command and which, on the other
hand, he prepares us to condone. One may get to the point "of
reading <u>Tom Jones</u> with fascinated curiosity, baffled to make
out what he [Fielding] really does think about...the Christian
command of chastity."[70] This ambiguity is due to Fielding's
capacity for seeing more than one moral code by which society
judges and is judged. Tom's sins are real, and their consequences are serious; on the other hand, Tom is not mean, and
his offenses, often the result of generous impulses, however
thoughtless, are the means of his achieving real understanding
of the necessity for prudence. Fielding's broad moral pers-
pective resulted in evaluations of a number of moral shortcomings; some marriage designs, Blifil's for instance, are
more vicious that profligacy.[71] Blifil's motive Fielding describes as that honorable intention of robbing a lady of her
fortune by marriage. But far more repugnant than his avarice
is his anticipation of the day when he will revenge Sophia's
rebuff with sexual cruelty (VII, 6). The relative nature of
Tom's shortcomings is further emphasized by a contrast with
Mr. B__'s and Lovelace's prolonged campaigns to commit
rape. Their fondling of the idea of conquest is far more reprehensible than Tom's actual sins, which are mainly spontaneous
responses to youthful impulse. Tom's realization that his own
follies, not the whims of Fortune, have nearly accomplished
his destruction is the most important step in his reformation.
It is to this point that the novel leads from the beginning. When

he achieves self-restraint and prudence, he is fit for marriage to Sophia. Fielding states the case in defense of a sinner, not a villain:

> a single bad act no more constitutes a villain in life, than a single bad part on the stage. The passions... often force men upon parts without consulting their judgment.... Thus the man...may condemn what he himself acts....the man of candour and true understanding can censure an imperfection, or even a vice, without rage at the guilty party (VII, 1).

So Tom's errors are condemned, but he is forgiven.

The same duality of standards noted in the moral evaluation of Tom affects the judging of Sophia's behavior. Although her disobedience to her father is not so grave an offense to the modern reader as Tom's sins, it was certainly a serious matter to eighteenth-century readers, who were themselves engrossed in real life with this changing pattern of conduct and relishing it in such fictional versions as Clarissa Harlowe's struggle. The denunciations of Sophia by contemporary critics, as few as they are and often motivated by old animosities toward the author, invariably attack the example of filial disobedience. They are rarely as scurrilous as the charge of a critic in the <u>Examen of Tom Jones</u> (1750) that Sophia is "trash";[72] more typical is the comment of Fielding's unrelenting rival, Samuel Richardson, who deplored, without reading the book, "so fond, so foolish, and so insipid" an heroine, "a Young Creature who was trapsing [sic] after him [Tom], a Fugitive from her Father's House."[73]

Fielding's description of Sophia as "a lady with whom we ourselves are greatly in love, and with whom many of our readers will probably be in love" (III, 10), might well extend to the critics, for excepting the handful of disparaging comments from his enemies, Sophia has rarely been censured. Richardson's criticism is less characteristic than the tribute to "the adorable Sophia" as a "charming example—the first of her race—of an unsentimentalized flesh-and-blood heroine."[74]

She embodies all the qualities of the author's ideal, based on
the model of his first wife. Book IV, Chapter 2 is an apostrophe not only to the beauty of Sophia, dazzling enough in itself,
but also to the inhabitant of that "beautiful frame." "Her mind
was every way equal to her person...when she smiled, the
sweetness of her temper diffused that glory over her countenance which no regularity of feature can give." Moreover,
all of her natural gifts have been improved by education. And
to the inestimable treasures of beauty, good-nature, charitable
disposition, and modesty which she will bring her husband, the
crowning jewel, in Allworthy's list of her qualities, is her
lack of "pertness, or what is called repartee." She makes

> no pretence to wit, much less to that kind of wisdom
> which is the result only of great learning and experience
> .... She has no dictatorial sentiments, no judicial opin-
> ions, no profound criticisms. Whenever...in the com-
> pany of men, she hath been all attention, with the mod-
> esty of a learner, not the forwardness of a teacher (XVII,
> 3).

In short, she is not a learned lady. (See Appendix C) Like all
Fielding's heroines, she is a man's woman—created to express
the charm that women have for men and not, like such later
creations as Austen's for example, made to be as endearing
t o women as to men. [75]
    If the acrimony involved in contemporary attacks is ignored,
there is still some solid basis for the inability of Richardson
and his adherents to admire the character of the lovely and
virtuous Sophia. For one thing, she completely rejects the
mercenary standards of Pamela; and although there are points
of agreement between the principles of Sophia and Clarissa
(Clarissa appeared the year before Tom Jones), their courses
of action are very different because of the different aims of the
two novelists. In her attitude toward both her parent and her
lover, Sophia is nearer the ideal of a modern girl than of an
eighteenth-century lady of either the sentimental or Restoration fashionable tradition. However, Sophia's struggles are

all presented in terms of Fielding's conviction that a woman's
proper role was one of submission to her husband; their relationship might be ideal, but the woman was nonetheless subordinate.   Clarissa, in many respects perfectly typical of the
sentimental tradition, is more modern in that she is struggling
primarily for self-realization.

The simple rule of filial obligation in the eighteenth century
commanded that a child obey the parent. Western's insistence
that in all matters the child should give "resigned obedience"
to the parent was not exceptional; he declares that he has bred
Sophia, and she is his to dispose of. Such views as Allworthy's
are a riddle to Western. Sophia, all of her girlhood years, has
observed her father's rule of filial duty, an obedience which
she describes as a delight having no equal. She plays his favorite jigs in preference to her own favorite, Handel; she rides
with him in the hunt, though she does not like the sport; in
brief, she acquiesces in whatever pleases him (IV, 10). Their
only disagreement before the marriage controversy has been
over Sophia's reluctance to second her father's condemnations
of her dead mother. When the squire extends the parental
right to an insistence that she marry a man she hates, Sophia
draws the line of obedience. She concedes the parent's right to
a negative voice, no more.

There is no hesitation in her resolve to flee in the middle
of the night and to face the perils of the road rather than accept matrimony with the detested Blifil. There is none of the
melancholy languishing in grief of the sentimental heroine; instead there is resolute action. Conscious that his heroine's
vigorous and independent behavior defies not only the custom
of the times regarding filial obligation but the tradition of the
passive, frail sentimental heroine as well, Fielding pauses in
the account of her flight to ridicule the "pretty arts which ladies sometimes practice to display their fears" and to commend
that courage "which not only becomes a woman, but is often
necessary to enable her to discharge her duty" (X, 9). It is
this kind of courage which enables Sophia, who has "all the
gentleness a woman can have," as well as "all the spirit which
she ought to have," to carry out her convictions. There are

none of the pretty arts of dissimulation in her conduct under the greatest stress. No clearer contrast between a Richardsonian heroine and a Fielding heroine could be found than in Pamela's resistance to Mr. B__'s attacks and Sophia's to Lord Fellamar. Pamela faints at the crucial moment; Sophia fights with a good deal of spirit. Sophia's fainting fits serve as a useful index to her character.[76] She does indeed faint, but on each occasion it is fear for others and not for herself which prompts her fainting, e.g. when she sees Tom injured and when she hears the false report of his death. Nor does she faint as sentimental ladies did, at the mere excess of emotional meditation. Sophia is in fact not afflicted with the eighteenth-century heroine's malady of self-analysis of emotions and sensibilities, though she loves to shed a tear now and again over a tender sensation in fiction (VI, 5).

Although Sophia is determined to resist marriage against her wishes, her dutiful offer to sacrifice her own inclinations if her father will allow her to return home and remain "his Sophia" for the rest of his life, leaves little room for censure. If any exists, it is removed by the irascibility of a father who reasons so illogically ("If she marries the man I would ha' her, she may love whom she pleases" [VI, 2]) and shows his love so perversely ("Will marriage kill you?.... Then die and be d—d" [VI, 7]).

One of the subtlest touches in the humanizing of Sophia occurs just before her flight. Her father, believing that she has consented to marry Blifil, showers her with kisses, embraces, and money. His unrestrained joy so moves her tender heart that she considers playing the role of martyr to filial love and duty. The idea of an action so heroic agreeably tickled her pride, says Fielding, but only for a moment—in that moment Fielding allows her to play the role of the popular sentimental heroine. Then he brings her back to sanity through the recollection of Tom, and "some hopes (however distant)...immediately destroyed all which filial love, piety and pride" tempted her to do (VII, 9).

What seems to be approval of the defeat of filial duty, piety and pride by love is of course approval only of Sophia's right

decision not to be ruined by parental injustice. She has secret
hopes regarding Tom, but in the present she is escaping Blifil.
Fielding realistically faced the consequences of defiance of
convention in other instances of filial defiance introduced into
the novel. The sad history of Mrs. Fitzpatrick is unfolded to
Sophia as a testament to the disastrous results of rashly marrying against the counsel of friends and relations (XI, 4-5).
From the Quaker, Tom hears a similar tale unfolded of a
father's determination to cast off a daughter who married
against his wishes (VII, 10). The girl's case so exactly parallels Sophia's that Tom cannot bear to hear the story to the end;
the reader is thus warned that not every romantic elopement
will have the happy ending that befalls Sophia and Tom. Mrs.
Fitzpatrick's actions are her undoing because, largely motivated by vanity, she chooses a knave interested only in her
money. The Quaker's daughter, like Sophia, faces ruin by a
father's obstinacy; both bestow their love upon a basically
worthy young man. The good fortune of Sophia owes more to
the intervention of the author than to any difference inherent in
their situation.

Sophia's conduct toward Tom is in some ways as far ahead
of the time as her attitude toward filial duty. First of all, she
is more concerned with the personal merit than the social
status of her lover. When she mistakenly assumes that her
aunt approves of Tom, she pours forth a eulogy of his virtues
and charms which to her more than compensate for social inequality. She would not hesitate to marry him, illegitimate
and without an inheritance, as she knows him to be. Moreover,
she is altogether too honest about her emotions for a young
lady of fashion. Once in love to distraction she cannot and
does not try to hide her feelings from Tom. After the match
with Blifil is proposed, she promises Tom that she will never
consent; her refusal to offer any hope to him, however, is un-
selfishly based on the realization of the misery she will cause
her father and the ruin she will bring on Tom.

Sophia's faithfulness and trust are especially notable in
view of the brevity of the time that the two have acknowledged
their love before the separation and the considerable grounds

Tom gives her to doubt his sincerity. Her seeming about-face after all the obstacles to their union are removed has been objected to by some critics who find this her only moment of coyness. Coleridge thought the dialogue in the reconciliation scene unrealistic. Watt finds Sophia's reversal sudden and unexplained, the scene having comic life at the expense of reality.[77] To this writer it seems perfect truth to female psychology. She would be less than human if she did not indulge in a moment of triumph after enduring so many trials and having her pride so battered. The recollection of Tom's conduct with Molly and Jenny and the more recent evidence of Tom's proposal of marriage to Lady Bellaston, though never seriously intended, rankles. She requires Tom to convince her of the constancy of his love. After all the assurances she could desire, she faces the dilemma of not wishing to give in too easily and at the same time desiring to marry him immediately. There is no surer touch in Fielding's portrayal of the feminine mind than in having Sophia allow her father to command her obedience in an immediate ceremony, which she eagerly grants this time. Since all parties wish the marriage to take place without delay, Tom and Sophia, unlike Joseph and Fanny, are married in a civil ceremony at Doctors'-Commons (XVIII, 13). As in the case of Joseph and Fanny, Fielding assures us that "there are not to be found a worthier man and woman, than this fond couple, so neither can any be imagined."

> Whatever in the nature of Jones had a tendency to vice, has been corrected by continual conversation with this good man [Allworthy], and by his union with the lovely and virtuous Sophia. He hath, also, by reflection on his past follies, acquired a discretion and prudence very uncommon in one of his lively parts (XVIII, 13).

"Whatever in the nature of Jones had a tendency to vice, has been corrected"—thus Fielding puts the seal upon the moral design of the novel.

We are glad to assume that they lived happily ever after, especially so since an ideal marriage in its day-by-day course

is not presented in the novel. As a comic novelist, Fielding
had no obligation to show in detail evidence of the happiness
which is bestowed upon the removal of the obstacles to the hero
and heroine and the accomplishment of their marriage. It is to
be his aim in Amelia to pick up the thread of experiences of a
worthy couple after marriage; and it is a novel which does not
adhere to the conventional pattern of comedy. In Tom Jones it
cannot be denied that the vivid marriages are far from idyllic.
Allworthy's and Mrs. Miller's marriages were happy ones, but
we never actually observe these. We were told that Allworthy
married a beautiful and worthy woman whom he loved so fond-
ly that after her death he spoke of himself as still married and
had not the least doubt that he would be reunited with her in
another life. Such sentiments, Fielding comments ironically,
caused his neighbors to question his sense, his religion, and
his sincerity (I, 2). Serving as a mentor character, Allworthy
gives the fullest exposition of Fielding's concept of marriage,
in his sermon on matrimony (I, 12):

> I have always thought love the only foundation of happi-
> ness in a married state, as it can only produce that high
> and tender friendship which should be the cement of this
> union; and, in my opinion, all those marriages which
> are contracted from other motives are greatly criminal
> .... To deny that beauty is an agreeable object to the eye
> ...would be false and foolish. But to make this the sole
> consideration of marriage, to lust after it so violently
> as...to reject and disdain religion, virtue, and sense,
> which are qualities in their nature of much higher per-
> fection...is surely inconsistent, either with a wise man
> or a good Christian.

Prudence, he concludes, requires some consideration of the
means for supporting a family, but marriage based on the desire to gratify vain indulgences and to augment fortune is folly.
Fielding invariably paid tribute to marriage between such
worthy individuals who based their marriage on love, religion,
virtue, and sense. In such a union each of the partners found-

ed his own happiness on the well-being and contentment of the other, and mutual trust was the bond of the union. The pleasures of domestic life superseded those of fashionable society.

Fielding's tributes to such ideal marriage, however, are not so vivid as his portraits, often in miniature, of ordinary mortals whose motives are less pure. The chief of these is Bridget's match with Captain Blifil. Bridget, a hypocritical prude past her bloom, is already the mother of Tom, when Blifil appears to court her, or more properly to court Allworthy's "house and gardens, his lands, tenements, and hereditaments" (I, 11). The first bliss of matrimony once past, the captain resumes his attitude that a woman is an animal of domestic use, of somewhat, though not much, higher consideration than a cat. He treats with haughtiness and insolence his wife's opinions, to which he had obligingly deferred before marriage. His indignities Bridget returns with contempt. The result is a marriage from which each derives the exquisite pleasure of tormenting the other (II, 7). The usual outlet for their disputes is taking opposite sides on every issue; thus Blifil's hatred of Tom evokes Bridget's tenderness to him in preference to her acknowledged child. The secret joy which sustains Blifil is the anticipation of the eventual inheritance of Allworthy's estate; during one of these pleasant meditations on the happiness to come, he dies of apoplexy, thereby regaining his wife's love (II, 8).

Squire Western's marriage provides a portrait of a pathetic wife married against her will by a "fond father" for financial gain. Her whimpering and whining before the marriage won her no more charity from her father than Sophia's tearful appeals do from Western (VI, 7). The squire, who regarded his wife as a faithful upper servant, fulfilled his own notion of a good husband: "he seldom swore at her (perhaps not above once a week) and never beat her." She had no occasion for jealousy and was the mistress of her time, since the squire spent his mornings in the field and his evenings with bottle companions and generally retired so drunk that he could not see. His wife did not make all the return he expected to so much indulgence, and her occasional interference "in the gen-

tlest terms" into matters that did not concern her, such as
the squire's violent drinking, finally resulted in his uncon-
cealed hatred of her. The marriage, which ended with the
wife's death when Sophia was eleven, is a memory which fur-
nishes the squire with inexhaustible material for invective; for
every disappointment, from a bad scenting day to distemper
among his hounds, he imagines would have afforded his wife
comfort (VII, 4).

Of the other marriages of which we have brief glimpses,
the general picture is one of discord and misery: the Fitzpatricks are motivated by vanity and avarice in a marriage that
finally ends in separation by mutual consent; the Partridges
live in a state of turmoil because of the wife's unfounded jealousy; the Seagrims, in misery because of Black George's inability to provide adequately for his brood. At the inn where
Jones is wounded by Northerton, the nagging landlady brow-
beats her present husband with constant encomiums on the
wisdom of her first husband. The most dismal circumstances
attend the marriage of Mrs. Miller's cousin, a love match.
The husband turns in desperation to robbing to obtain necessities for his family. Tom, one of his intended victims, endears
himself to the entire family by aiding them in their distress.
Mrs. Miller uses the woes of this couple as a warning to her
own daughters against marrying without a competency (XIII, 8).
Whether or not by explicit design, Fielding has portrayed an
assortment of unsatisfactory marriages which illustrate a
variety of ills: mercenary motives, avarice, vanity, jealousy,
poverty, and contrariness.

The matchmaking which is a part of the final meting out of
rewards (and punishments) in the concluding chapter is a
forceful reminder that Fielding is a humorous writer with
strong proclivities to farce. In an outburst of exuberant good-
nature, which Sherburn notes as frequently affecting English
authors (even Shakespeare) at a joyful conclusion,[78] Fielding
lets the spirit of fun run rampant in a set of unions that could
have been devised only tongue in cheek. Blifil's courtship of
and likely marriage to a Methodist widow, a fate adequate for
such a villain as Blifil, is a blast at a sect that Fielding heart-

ily disliked. His disposal of Mrs. Waters and Molly borders
on the farcical. In marrying Jenny Waters to Parson Supple,
he is pairing off a woman of casual virtue with a curate in a
match hardly made in heaven or likely to produce much bliss
on earth. Plans are on foot, with the mediation of none other
than Sophia, for a match between Partridge and Molly. Partridge, the long-sufferer from a jealous first wife, is now about
to take a wife of less than half his age with something more
than a casual predisposition toward mankind en masse. These
unlikely couples have the blessings of Allworthy, Western,
Tom, and Sophia. Surely Fielding himself enjoyed a hearty
laugh as he bestowed Tom's former lovers around him as his
neighbors. The ending is reminiscent of the spirit of the reconciliation scenes which conclude many Renaissance comedies
with a literal refrain: "Let's all join hands and dance and sing
—old differences are forgotten."

From the array of ill-assorted marriages presented in the
novel in contrast with that of Tom and Sophia, it is the unavoid-
able conclusion that Fielding considered ideal marriages ex-
ceedingly rare. Such a marriage would require two worthy
partners who base their marriage on the highest concept of
Christian love and merit; consent of the parents or guardians
is desirable; and a comfortable income to provide adequately
for the family is necessary. Significantly, class structure is
maintained.

Fielding provides the desired conditions for his lovers at
the point of their marriage, but the reader is no more blind
than Fielding was to the difficulty of achieving all these conditions in the world of reality. The reluctance of many readers
to accept Tom's reformation, and in <u>Amelia</u> Booth's conversion, is the result of the nearly impossible task of the comic,
and especially the satiric, writer to meld perfectly the moral
scheme and the traditional plot elements of comedy, most evident in the contrived conclusion. The contrast is more
marked in <u>Amelia</u> because of the increased seriousness of the
subject and the abandonment of the humor characteristic of
<u>Joseph Andrews</u> and <u>Tom Jones</u>. In an excellent analysis, Ian
Watt declares <u>Tom Jones</u> to be the pinnacle of Fielding's hum-

or having as its basis the tacit assumption of broad-minded-
ness in its modern sense, which tends to have a sexual reference, and

> is part of the expansion of sympathy to which his novels
> as a whole invite us: a relish for wholesome bawdy, in
> fact, is a necessary part of the moral education of a sex-
> bedevilled humanity: such at least was the classical role
> of comedy, and Fielding was perhaps the last great writ-
> er who continued that tradition. [79]

It might be added that <u>Tom Jones</u> is the last novel in which
Fielding practiced this tradition, for it is a different art which
characterizes his story of the grim struggle of Amelia and
Billy Booth to make their way in a world that has little mercy
to offer those without means.

Chapter 5

MARRIAGE IN THE LATER NOVELS:
AMELIA

"And so they were married" is the usual signal for ringing down the curtain on adventures in fiction, but as the first reviewer of Amelia noted, Fielding makes the bold stroke of beginning his narrative where most novels leave off. [80] Amelia is the first effort in English fiction to study realistically the problems of marriage. (Pamela, Part II, which preceded Amelia, purports to be the story of the B__s' marriage; actually it ceases to be a novel and becomes little more than a conduct book in dialogue form.) Amelia completes the picture of marriage in Fielding's work, as it also rounds out the portrait of the man behind the novels. We would not fully understand Fielding without it.

The exuberant romantic faculty of Joseph Andrews... the mighty craftsmanship and the vast science of life of Tom Jones; the ineffable irony and logical grasp of Jonathan Wild, might have left us with a slight sense of hardness ... if it had not been for the completion of the picture. [81]

Amelia has rarely been the choice of critics or of general readers as Fielding's greatest novel, the preference usually being given to Tom Jones as the novel that holds in most nearly perfect equilibrium the various elements of fiction. Just as irony swings the balance in Jonathan Wild, so the moralistic purpose does in Amelia. Baker describes Amelia as the ugly truth stated literally, "not hinted with luminous and delightful indirectness; denounced, rather than held up to ridicule." [82]

The change to a wholly serious manner in moral purpose and
narrative technique, Rawson attributes to a deep alteration in
Fielding's own vision. "Brutal forces of an absurd universe
meet the Augustan rage for order face to face," and the result
of this confrontation for an increasingly pessimistic Fielding
is loss of faith in an ordered world. [83] As Sherburn adds,
some surprise and disappointment usually follow any work of
an established author who suddenly changes his tone or technique.[84] Certainly Amelia has continued to be a surprise and
disappointment to modern readers as much as to Fielding's
contemporaries as they have tried to reconcile its sombre
qualities with the broad burlesque humor of the parodies and
the high comedy of Tom Jones. It has met more variable and
contradictory criticism from its publication to the present than
any other of Fielding's novels.

The bases of the major contemporary objections to the novel
are fundamental to Fielding's portrait of marriage and thus
merit a more detailed account than has been given in this study
to the critical reception of the other works. That the novel
was Fielding's "favorite child" we know from his moving defense of it in the trial of the book described in The Covent-
Garden Journal. [85] On it, he says, he lavished "more than
ordinary pains." Its message was the earnest conviction of
one who saw and deplored man's inhumanity to his fellows.
He wrote this last plea in behalf of humanity in spite of the
press of magisterial duties which left him spent and in spite
of the increasing painfulness of his disease. The rancour and
ridicule which greeted this effort, so close to his heart,
prompted the declaration that he would trouble the world no
more with any "children" of his by the same Muse. Amelia
was subjected to the cruelest abuse suffered by the author in a
career marked from the beginning by the scurrility of the attacks. [86] Although the abuse was undeserved, the book unfortunately lent itself to ridicule more readily than any other
of Fielding's writing. Enemies pounced gleefully on the oversight of Fielding in failing to mend Amelia's broken nose (II, 1).
The slip was corrected in the second edition, but this revision
did not appear in the author's lifetime. Besides, the damage

was done; the opportunity for vengeance was too sweet—and easy—to be missed. Slurs on Amelia's character to account for her noselessness were common. [87] Amelia's "vile broken nose," as Samuel Johnson described it, injured the reputation of the book for contemporary readers and converted the purest of Fielding's heroines into a subject for coarse jest. Even the choice of her name was unfortunate; its parody form of Shamelia was too apt to be overlooked.

Although there was much ado about Amelia's nose, certainly more than the oversight deserved, there were criticisms of the book and its characters other than those motivated by the desire to settle old scores. Even the commendatory reviews agreed with the less favorable but not hostile accounts in pointing out certain objections. The theme of the attacks is set by the first review, though it has only praise for the author's high purpose, with the complaint that the sordidness of characters and situations is "too long dwelt on."[88] The denunciations rely heavily on the adjective low. Fielding uses it six times in quoting the charges brought against the book: Amelia, Colonel Bath, and Dr. Harrison are "low" characters, and the scenes are likewise "low." His intent was ironic, of course, but there is accuracy in his summary of the complaints.

Samuel Richardson, gleeful over the adverse reception, [89] dismissed the characters as so "wretchedly low and dirty" that he is compelled to ask, "Who can care for any of his people?"[90] —a judgment echoed by Richardson's adherents. Richardson's proclamation, while it was no doubt prompted by a wrath against Fielding which he had nursed through the years to keep it warm, expressed not merely the view of his sentimental followers but of a reading public to whom frank and sober realism was not yet acceptable. Richardson's antipathy was not softened even by Fielding's praise of Clarissa (The Jacobite's Journal, January 2, 1747-48). In Fielding's words, Amelia was brought to the bar for "daring to stand up in opposition to the humour of the age."[91] The book defied the humor of the age basically in its portrayal of the chief characters and in the grimness of the distresses through which Fielding has them "wade." Moreover, though the objection is not so explicitly stated, there is dissatisfaction with Booth that has persisted through the years; whereas Amelia has come into her own as one of the noblest heroines in English fiction.[92] The rejection of Booth results in some measure from failure to understand Fielding's purpose in the portrayal of the hero and in the novel as a whole; in part from Fielding's failure to accomplish that purpose fully.

In Tom Jones's struggle to become worthy of marriage to Sophia, as we have seen, Fielding has the youth face the social obstacles of illegitimacy and lack of wealth and along with them the personal conflicts involved in learning prudence and practicing self-discipline based on Christian precepts. Similarly in Amelia Fielding builds his plot situation of "the various accidents which befel a very worthy couple after their uniting in the state of matrimony" (I,1) around a moral problem which Sherburn calls "almost a fantasy on the subject of the Stoic and Christian attitudes toward conduct."[93] The preoccupation with the distresses which they waded through often obscures the fact that a fully successful marriage is impossible, despite Amelia's perfection as a wife, until Booth is converted to Christianity and discards the false doctrine that men act from their predominant passion (I,1) and its corollary that moral struggle is futile. Work sees Tom Jones as primarily a good man on the purely human level. But by the time Fielding wrote Amelia, he felt that something stronger than Tom's mere benevolence was needed; so, continues Work, he provided a conversion and Dr. Harrison's preachments on the hope of heaven and the fear of hell.[94] To bring Booth to full moral maturity, Fielding must trace his inability to master the Art of Life until he gains the moral strength "to retrieve the ill consequences of a foolish conduct, and by struggling manfully with distress to subdue it...one of the noblest efforts of wisdom and virtue" (I,1). Further, like Tom, Booth must see that his own follies, not Fortune, are the cause of most of his misfortunes. In no other of his novels does Fielding make so overt a statement of the intent of his work.

In Amelia, as in every other novel by Fielding, there are a multiplicity of subordinate episodes which, at the same time

that they enrich the novel, serve to blur the central problem.
In accord with Fielding's own division, Sherburn groups these
into social and personal themes.[95] Fielding states in the Dedication that he wishes "to expose some of the most glaring
evils, as well public as private, which at present infest the
country." These public evils are various, but they all contribute to corruption in society; the privileged classes especially come under attack as responsible for the degradation of
the age because they do not provide recognition for merit and
incentive to honesty.[96] It is against the injustices and immorality of this society, largely contemptuous of religion,
that husband and wife struggle. Their personal conflicts are
intensified by the social evils. Much of the material of the
novel does not properly fall within the limits of this study,
which will examine only those situations relevant to the marriage question. Fielding states fully his mature view of marriage as he examines in detail the background of the Booths'
courtship, their qualifications for marriage, and their manage-
ment of the crises they face after marriage.

As the obstacle to their courtship and marriage, Amelia
and Booth face the standby plot complication of fiction: the
opposition of a parent on financial grounds (See Book II, 1-8
for the full account of the courtship.) Booth first regards
Amelia "in the dawn of her beauty" with admiration based on
the general esteem shown for her by people of high rank. He
considers her out of the reach of an ensign whose sole income
is his pay as a soldier and whose hopes for advancement are
precarious. The first spark of feeling deeper than admiration
is aroused by the accident which temporarily mars her beauty
and makes her a figure of ridicule to her superficial friends
and suitors. Sympathy and admiration deepen into love; it is
a love based on the superiority of her mind and character, not
on her physical beauty. A marriage based on this kind of love,
which Fielding repeatedly extolled, should have prospered,
given a fair chance, and in the end the Booths' does succeed.

It is the sympathetic impulse of Booth's generous nature that
inspires Amelia's first response to him. The realization that
his feelings are fully shared leads Booth to a futile attempt to

disguise his love in order to save Amelia from the difficulties
he foresees for her as his wife—separation from her husband
and possibly his loss in battle, poverty as the patrimony of
their children, and alienation from her mother, who is certain
to oppose so disadvantageous a match. Amelia nevertheless
vows her love for him. Discovery by Mrs. Harris and temporary separation are followed by Dr. Harrison's intervention on
the lovers' behalf and the mother's reluctant consent. The joy
of the lovers and unfortunately the legal proceedings for the
marriage settlement are interrupted by Booth's absence at the
bedside of his dying sister. During the interval, a Mr. Winckworth arrives with coach and six and the offer of an advantageous match for Amelia. Mrs. Harris ignores the prior contract and accepts Winckworth for Amelia. Amelia's refusal of
the new suitor is seconded forcefully by Dr. Harrison, who insists that she is bound by the promise to Booth and that the two
are as much man and wife as if the ceremony had already occurred. This is Fielding's most explicit use of the old tradition of <u>sponsalia per verba de futuro</u> as a binding vow. It was
not technically the equivalent of marriage unless consummation
followed the vow; however, the agreement was legally binding
unless both parties consented to its cancellation or one party
gave just cause for breaking the vow. (See Appendix A.)

Dr. Harrison condemns the suitor for paying addresses to
another man's wife, but Winckworth is too much enamoured to
regard the minister's attacks. Mrs. Harris' obduracy removes any obligation to her, and Dr. Harrison himself proposes to procure a license and perform the ceremony without
parental consent, "which every parent, he said, had a right to
refuse, but not to retract when given, unless the party himself,
by some conduct of his gave a reason" (II, 5). Mrs. Harris is
at last frightened into compliance by the clergyman's determination to assist Amelia and Booth. The two are married by
license, in church, with the consent, reluctant though it is, of
the parent.

Fielding gives fuller attention in this episode to the legal
steps involved in matrimony than in any other of the novels.
He emphasizes the moral obligations of all parties: it is the
duty of the child to seek the parent's consent; the parent also

has the duty of allowing the child some voice. There are circumstances when it is right to disobey the parent. Fielding, however, is careful to base his lovers' case on valid legal grounds as well as moral; Mrs. Harris's objections, if allowed to prevail, would have nullified a binding agreement and the support of her own and the young couple's spiritual adviser.

Once married, the Booths face almost immediately the difficulties Booth had foreseen. These problems on one level center around his inability to support his family. After a brief service with the army at the siege of Gibraltar, Booth is cashiered on half-pay. In spite of his real merit as a soldier, he cannot advance except by purchase of a commission. Before her sudden death, Mrs. Harris had neglected to settle the sum promised for such purchase; and Amelia is cheated of her inheritance by the manipulations of her sister Betty and the lawyer Murphy in executing a fraudulent will. The Booths find themselves nearly penniless. Dr. Harrison's efforts to set them up in the country fail when Booth succumbs to vanity and poses as a gentleman instead of a mere farmer. Ruin follows fast, and Booth flees to London to escape the debts which he cannot pay. Here, through a gross miscarriage of justice, he is arrested for trying to help a fellow in distress. His imprisonment involves him with Miss Matthews, who provides money for his freedom. One failure leads to another as Booth, confined to the verge of court, seeks some means to extricate himself from debt and regain a livelihood. He feeds on the air, promise-crammed by men whose real motive is the pursuit of his wife. Much of the weakness attributed to Booth by critics is rather Fielding's condemnation of that class who have the means at their disposal to recognize and provide for merit but who instead are motivated by self-interest or are carelessly indifferent.

Indeed, the way of advancement is always open at the price of Amelia's honor. Thus the financial difficulties of the Booths merge with their moral problems. Here Fielding develops some of the situations used earlier in The Modern Husband (1732). The central situation of the devoted husband, Bellamant-Booth, who has been guilty of infidelity to a virtuous and

forgiving wife, Mrs. Bellamant-Amelia, is the same. Miss
Matthews and Mrs. Trent combine the role of Mrs. Modern.
The scabrous theme, as Baker calls it, of the pimping husband,
Mr. Modern-Trent, has a subordinate place in Amelia and
serves as the climax of the stratagems of the unscrupulous
peer, Lord Richly of the play.

A. R. Towers considers the heart of Fielding's treatment of
marriage in Amelia to be the question of adultery. [97] It is
true that much of the plot complication stems from the temptations faced by both Amelia and Booth. Amelia is beset almost from the beginning of her marriage by amorous advances,
first from Monsieur Bagillard and later from James and the
peer in prolonged and carefully planned schemes. With great
discretion Amelia spurns Bagillard and James, without letting
Booth know of either, though in both cases she suffers by her
silence. It seems likely that the subtler schemes of the peer,
who has completely disarmed Amelia, might have succeeded
except for Mrs. Bennet's intervention.

Although Booth's infidelity with Miss Matthews, particularly reprehensible when set against Amelia's steadfast loyalty,
tries the marriage sorely, that offense in itself is not the thing
which almost wrecks the marriage. Amelia, who learned of
the affair long before the remorseful Booth made his confession, has forgiven and all but forgotten the lapse. By having
Amelia forgive Booth in advance, Fielding does not imply the
condoning of adultery, any more than he had done so in Tom
Jones. In fact, Dr. Harrison voices Fielding's most vehement
condemnation of "the great sin of adultery": [98]

Hath the government provided any law to punish it? Or
doth the priest take any care to correct it? On the contrary, is the most notorious practice of it any detriment
to a man's fortune or to his reputation in the world? doth
it exclude him from any preferment in the State, I had
almost said the Church? is it any blot in his escutcheon?
any bar to his honour? is he not to be found every day in
the assemblies of women of the highest quality? in the
closets of the greatest men, and even at the tables of

bishops? What wonder then if the community in general
treat this monstrous crime as a matter of jest, and that
men give way to the temptations of a violent appetite,
when the indulgence of it is protected by law and coun-
tenanced by custom (IX, 5)?

Baker sees the tragic irony of marital distrust rather than
infidelity as the cause that almost undoes the marriage. [99] As
Booth cannot bring himself because of fear and pride to con-
fess his lapse, so Amelia fails to confide the real motive behind James's pretense of friendship because she fears Booth
will make a hot-headed assault on James. Thus the two work
unconsciously against each other.

Since all the crises, financial and moral, inevitably evoke
a comparison between the husband and wife, a more detailed
examination of the qualities of each will be made. Amelia,
"the most real of all Fielding's characters,"[100] has been the
object of admiration to those who agree with her husband's estimate that she has every perfection in human nature (III, 1).
Even Samuel Johnson, who had few kind words for Fielding,
thought Amelia attractive. Scott found the book unpleasing, but
the heroine amiable. Thackeray's enthusiasm is obvious in the
use of her name and good qualities, but sadly not her spirit, in
his own Amelia Sedley. [101] That her goodness palls on some
readers, however, is clear in Saintsbury's faint praise. He
defends the novel against the charge that it reveals a falling off
of power and vitality, [102] but he feels that though Amelia is not
the amiable fool her namesake in <u>Vanity Fair</u> seems to be, she
has "too much of the milk of human kindness unrefreshed and
unrelieved of its mawkishness by the rum or whisky of human
frailty, in her." So recent a critic as F.R. Leavis, in a rather summary dismissal of Fielding's career, declares that "by
<u>Amelia</u> Fielding has gone soft."[103] He does not specify what
aspect of the novel—character, incident, technique, or the
whole—accounts for the judgment;[104] however, in view of the
increased seriousness of tone and purpose and the grimness of
the subject and scenes, it is perhaps logical to conclude that

Leavis' judgment is made in terms of the greater degree of
sentimentalism and sensibility, especially evident in Booth,
than is found in the earlier novels. These, at least, are the
qualities most likely to be objectionable to modern readers;
Fielding's contemporaries condemned the Booths primarily for
their failure to observe the standards of fashionable society.
By such standards, Amelia is

> a low character, a Fool, a Milksop...she shows too much
> kindness for her husband. ...she exerts no Manner of
> Spirit, unless, perhaps in the supporting Afflictions...
> her not abusing him [Booth]...when she saw his Heart
> was already almost broke...was contemptible Meanness
> ...she dresses her Husband's Supper; dresses her chil-
> dren; and submits to the thoughts of every servile of-
> fice. [105]

Amelia fulfilled the role of sentimental heroine no better
than that of the woman of fashion to the taste of her own day,
though she does reveal a degree of sensibility far greater than
Sophia's. Utter and Needham attribute Amelia's increased
tendency to tearfulness and swooning—four times to Sophia's
one—to be the pressures of poverty, childbearing, and anxiety. [106] However, the element of sentimentality cannot be wholly discounted; Amelia faints a number of times before marriage and the cause is often merely excessive emotionalism,
not as with Sophia, concern for the safety of others. The same
tendency toward extreme sensibility is present in Booth, to an
even greater degree than in Amelia and far beyond anything in
Fielding's earlier heroes. In his tearfulness he is clearly in
the tradition of the man of feeling who was to shed copious
tears on through the literature of the early nineteenth century.
Although given somewhat to tears and swoons, Amelia is in no
other way typical of the sentimental heroine. She acts vigorously in the face of every real crisis and never wallows in
melancholy meditation for its own sake. Her efforts are directed always outside herself to the care and comfort of her

husband and chilren.

Towers considers <u>Amelia</u> in relation to the tradition of conduct literature which was especially popular in the seventeenth
and eighteenth centuries and labels the novel a part of a "literary programme designed to glorify the pleasures of conjugal
love."[107] Thus the problems posed by Booth are so many opportunities to "provoke wifely responses of one sort or another
in Amelia. These responses are always in terms of the conventional but enlightened opinion of the age; taken together,
they form a picture of idealized conjugal behaviour."[108] This
is altogether too restrictive a definition of Fielding's aims in
the novel, even if consideration is limited to matrimonial issues. It reduces Amelia to less than the human and noble figure she is. For, though it is true that she is an ideal wife and
mother, she is far more than an examplary figure out of the
conduct book tradition. This interpretation ignores the fact
that the responses she makes to her problems were not those
acceptable to many of Fielding's contemporaries; much of the
adverse criticism came from those who certainly could be
characterized as conventional, though whether enlightened
might be debated. Conduct books might recommend certain
virtues, and Amelia varies little from the ideal as old as the
conception of a wife as a helpmeet and subordinate of the husband, but the heroine of popular fiction was not the equivalent
of the conduct book model.

Amelia defies both the precepts of the conduct books and the
standards of fashionable society when she marries against the
desire of the parent, for love rather than financial gain. She
is not at all concerned with making a figure in the world. She
declares herself content in any state, provided she has her
husband and her children. There is "no happiness out of his
company, nor scarce any misery in it" (IV, 3; IV, 9). She is
willing to rear her children to a humble station in life, in which
she foresees greater contentment than in the quest of vain
pleasures. She is obedient to her husband's will and restrains
any opposition at least until they are in private. As a housewife, she is depicted often in the process of preparing meals,
cheerful at her tasks (IV, 4). She is a good-natured hostess

without any "paltry pride" because of their reduced circumstances; not even unexpected guests of rank and wealth dis-
concert her. Her fondness for her children is complemented
by her efforts to nurture their spiritual as well as physical
needs.

> She never let a day pass without instructing her children
> in some lesson of religion and morality...she had in
> their tender minds so strongly annexed the ideas of fear
> and shame to every idea of evil, of which they were sus-
> ceptible, that it must require great pains and length of
> habit to separate them...she never suffered any symp-
> toms of malevolence to show itself in their most trifling
> actions without rebuke, and if it broke forth with any
> rancour, without punishment (IV, 3).

Dr. Harrison describes Amelia as having a "sweetness of
temper, a generosity of spirit, an openness of heart—in a
word...a true Christian disposition" (VIII, 8). Fielding is
careful to humanize Amelia by giving her some frailties. She
is not without vanity. Mrs. Bennet and Amelia are one day
discussing the folly of their sex in wishing above all else to be
handsome, whereupon both "fixed their eyes on the glass, and
both smiled" (VII, 3). She is a doting mother, allowing herself to be misled by the peer because of his flattery of her
children. Obedient to her husband's will in public, she does
not let him entirely escape private correction. On one occasion she acquieses when he opposes her attendance at a mas-
querade with Mrs. Ellison; privately she assures him she can
perform the duty of a wife to be silent and "the most miserable
of women" unless he will tell her the reason for his obstinate-
ness. He teases her, "That is...in other words...to say, I
will be contented without the secret but I am resolved to know
it, nevertheless" (XII, 6).
    Amelia's goodness and amiability are highlighted when she
is contrasted with Miss Matthews, in whom there is a generous quantity of that "rum or whisky of human frailty" Saintsbury found lacking in Amelia. He suggests that Fielding kept

Miss Matthews at a distance in the later portion of the novel "because he could not trust himself not to make her more interesting than Amelia."[109] Miss Matthews is indeed colorful, even flamboyant, and much can be said for her seeming generosity and spirit. There is the ring of magnificence in her declaration, "I would sacrifice the whole world at the least call of my love" (IV, 1). But she is also a woman of uncontrolled passion who does not hesitate to destroy the object of such love. She is careless of the moral laws she flouts. Vanity, assisted by hatred for her brother and jealousy of her sister, motivates her involvement with Hebbers. Her complete surrender to whatever passion rules at a moment results in her attempt to murder Hebbers, her violent love for Booth, and her subsequent revenge on Booth by alientating James. Her generosity to Booth is accompanied by protests that "love never confers any obligations. It doth everything for its own sake" (IV, 2). The nobility of the sentiment is not matched by her conduct, for she sets out to ruin Booth when he fails to fulfill the obligation she has placed him under.

She is one of Fielding's most successful creations of mixed character. She has keen insight; she almost instantly perceives the sensitive nature of Atkinson, to which Booth is unbelievably blind. Her willingness to give all for love is impressive, as inadequate as her understanding of that sentiment is. Amelia and Miss Matthews meet only once, at the prison, and Miss Matthews is vanquished by Amelia's goodness and generosity, which make her intolerable to Miss Matthews (IV, 2). It is a meeting which suggests that Fielding could safely have allowed her to enter the later action of the novel without overshadowing Amelia.

Fielding's portrait of Amelia as a paragon of feminine virtue but also a warm human creature is eminently successful. He was not so successful in drawing Billy Booth. When Baker declares the hero to be entirely of secondary importance,[110] he is stating a commonplace of criticism. This dismissal of Booth as insignificant is part of the failure to see to the heart of Fielding's purpose in the novel. Amelia is indeed its glory, but she is drawn entirely in relation to her husband. It is ac-

tually to Booth that all discussion of the novel leads: his character, his errors of judgment, and his conversion are the bases of the action. Amelia is the stable, or static, character
against whom the storms of adversity beat.[111] Towers sums
up their relationship thus: "Throughout the novel Booth constantly poses the problems of marriage while Amelia just as
regularly provides the solutions."[112] Like the view of Amelia
as a mere exemplary character, this evaluation fails to estimate the full role which Booth plays or to do credit to the
case which Fielding presents for him. Moreover, Amelia
would be more accurately described as enduring than solving
the problems posed by Booth.

Although Fielding called the novel Amelia rather than Billy
Booth, this is not a conclusive argument that the title figure of
the novel is the figure of central importance. Digeon suggests
that the real defect of Fielding's method in Amelia is the division of interest and action between Amelia and Booth.[113] The
reader cares more about Amelia, but the action turns on Booth.
Like Towers, Digeon places more emphasis than is justifiable
on Amelia's part in extricating Booth from his difficulties.

In addition to the division of the center of interest and the
center of action, Fielding inevitably damages his own case for
Booth by portraying his every flaw or error against the unfail-
ing goodness and generosity of Amelia. Moreover, it is somewhat difficult to swallow Amelia's statement that her understanding is inferior to her husband's when Dr. Harrison constantly relies on her good sense rather than Booth's. Even
here, however, it can be argued that Dr. Harrison has known
Amelia from her childhood; he knows Booth so little that even
in the concluding chapter he confesses his ignorance of Booth's
religious doubts. It cannot be denied that Booth stands in the
shadow of Amelia; this, however, is as much a measure of
her greatness as of Booth's inadequacy.

It is on the adequacy or inadequacy of Booth that the novel
succeeds or fails for the reader. His is the central problem
of the novel. He hardly deserves the epithets of inept, silly,
and stupid which are sometimes bestowed on him. Nor is he
a "weaker and unwiser Jones, considerably older."[114] Both

characters suffer from the comparison. By it, Tom is assumed to have only temporarily reformed; Booth, to be guilty
of behavior excusable only in an immature youth. The basic
difference in their characters makes these assumptions false.
Tom never wrestles with religious doubt; he declares himself,
though a sinner, at bottom a Christian. Booth is a skeptic;
unlike Tom, he is without the moral courage to accept his misfortunes as a result of his own failings. He must be brought to
the realization of individual moral responsibility. Moreover,
on the purely social level, Booth has been bred a gentleman,
though in reduced circumstances, and he struggles against
codes of fashionable behavior Tom did not face. Living in the
secluded scene, Tom for example has not been brought up to
such gentleman's failings as gambling.

Fielding's Booth, rather than the creation of the critics, is
a man of good and gentle disposition, a devoted husband, a kind
and jolly father, and a generous fellow by instinct. Banerji
objects that we do not see much proof of this generosity. He
cites only the opening incident when Booth rushes to the rescue
of the underdog, a stranger to him.[115] He neglects the generosity to an old soldier, whom he feeds and gives a small sum
of money, which he can certainly ill afford. Generosity,
moreover, need not be limited to such instances of material
proof. Concern for others is exhibited on many occasions. He
is present at the birth of the second child and cares for Amelia
with great tenderness. It is this same impulse of sympathy
that makes him so tender of Miss Matthews's situation and
leads him into entanglement with her.

His shortcomings, when enumerated, are not so great. He
is arrested three times: the first time for lending assistance
to a helpless man; the second time as much through the malice
of his neighbors as for his own folly; the third time by the
trickery of Trent, since debts of honor were not actionable in
law. He gambles once, with serious results, through the mach-
inations of Trent as an agent for the peer. Amelia pawns
clothes and trinkets to repay the debt, but Booth loses the
money in an effort to bribe the great man in the war office for
a commission. He does so on the recommendation of the old

soldier and with Amelia's approval. This latter incident is not so much a condemnation of Booth's judgment as a denunciation of the practice of touching. Booth, like many of his contemporaries, found the only hope of a livelihood through the practice. His desperation is such that he chases every chimera which promises a solution to his situation.

As for his moral lapse, "no man of his station (except Sir Charles Grandison)," declares Sherburn, "could have refused the overtures of Miss Matthews in Newgate."[116] There is no evidence that he has ever been unfaithful before, and his remorse and eagerness to break off the affair are convincing testimony that "though not absolutely a Joseph, as we have already seen, yet could he not be guilty of premeditated inconstancy" (X, 2).

The essential goodness of Booth is more adequately realized if he is contrasted with other gentlemen of his approximate class, particularly James, the peer, and Trent. Booth's immorality appears minor when placed against the moral shortcomings of these men. The effect is somewhat the same as that suggested in this study between Tom's lapses and the efforts to commit rape by Richardson's Mr. B__ and Lovelace and by Fielding's Lord Fellamar. The debate between Booth and James on the nature of love (V, 9) points up the difference between the two men. James's only concept of love is an appetite to be satisfied. The prospect of confining that appetite to one woman fills him with horror; such a life, he says, would be a damnable state. Booth assures him that he has never tired of his wife's company nor wished for any other's, for love is the object of love. The unnamed peer's profligacy is, as Booth tells Trent, "human nature depraved, stripped of all its worth, and loveliness, and dignity, and degraded down to a level with the vilest brutes" (X, 8). The peer employs his cast-off mistress Mrs. Trent and her husband, as well as Mrs. Ellison, as his agents; he pays well for the conquest of the victim, which is his only goal. The reader can see that if Booth had been in possession of an adequate income, most of his follies and the affair with Miss Matthews would never have occurred. There is none of the depravity of James and the

peer nor the avarice of the pimping husband in Booth's acts.
His errors resulted from his impecunious situation more than
from any inherent weakness. Fielding portrayed him in the
vise of circumstances.

Booth's shortcomings may be summed up as exemplifica-
tions of Dr. Harrison's statement that most of the ills of men
result from "bad education, bad habits, and bad customs."
Booth is well read, especially in the classics, but his knowledge is not deep enough. His inadequate intellectual training
leads to bad habits and following bad customs—purchase of the
coach, gambling, bribery—all follies of the age. The corrective which is necessary to complete his education is of a
Christian nature. [117]

It seems clear that Fielding intended Booth's physical imprisonments as a symbol of his spiritual confinement; for
when Booth reveals his conversion to true faith, Dr. Harrison
declares, "...as the devil hath thought proper to set you free,
I will try if I can prevail on the bailiff to do the same" (XII, 5).
The steps to this conversion, as well as the action of the entire
novel, center around Booth's three imprisonments. Arrested
unjustly on the first occasion, Booth is stripped of his coat by
his fellow prisoners when he fails to provide garnish. In his
dejected state, Booth "summoned his philosophy, of which he
had no inconsiderable share, to his assistance, and resolved
to make himself as easy as possible under his present circumstances" (I, 3). He and a sympathetic fellow prisoner, Robinson, shortly fall to debating the motivating force in life. Robinson argues that what is, is; what must be, must be: all
things happen by an inevitable fatality. Booth's sentiments
very nearly coincide with those of Robinson, whom Fielding
calls a deist, a free thinker, or perhaps an atheist. Fielding's
repudiation of deism is implicit in his associating it with athe-
ism. [118] Although Booth did not, with the fatalists, deny absolutely the existence of a God, he was in agreement with them
in denying His providence. Booth was a well-wisher to religion, but, by his own admission, his notions of it were slight
and uncertain. Booth's "wavering condition" Fielding likens
to that of Claudian:

> Then in turn my belief in God was weakened and failed, and
> even against mine own will I embraced the tenets of that
> other philosophy [Epicureanism] which teaches that atoms
> drift in purposeless motion and that new forms through-
> out the vast void are shaped by chance and not design—
> that philosophy which believes in God in an ambiguous
> sense, or holds that there be no gods, or that they are
> careless of our doings. [119]

The share of misfortunes, far greater than Booth felt he had
merited, added to his lack of religious conviction, led him into this "dangerous way of reasoning." In this wavering state,
Booth agrees with Robinson that human actions are the result
of necessity; however, he supports the belief that they arise
not from the impulse of fate but from the impulse of whatever
passion is uppermost in a man's mind (I, 3).

Following this false philosophy, Booth judges Colonel James
to be the highest recommendation of the doctrine of the passions. James never acts from motives of virtue or religion
and constantly laughs at both. "Yet his conduct toward me,"
declares Booth, "alone demonstrates a degree of goodness,
perhaps, few of the votaries of either virtue or religion can
equal" (III, 5). But Fielding says of James that in reality

> though a very generous man, [he] had not the least grain
> of tenderness in his disposition. His mind was formed
> of those firm materials of which nature formerly ham-
> mered out the Stoic, and upon whom the sorrows of no
> man living could make an impression. A man of this
> temper, who doth not much value danger, will fight for
> the person he calls his friend, and the man that hath but
> little value for his money will give it to him; but such
> friendship is never to be absolutely depended on; for
> whenever the favourite passion interposes with it, it is
> sure to subside and vanish into air (VIII, 5).

James is thus able to assume without any premeditated guile
the role of the "pleasantest of companions and one of the best-
natured men in the world," to care for the wounded Booth with

great concern, and to assist Booth generously with money. However, when lust for Miss Matthews and later for Amelia becomes the predominant passion, he just as easily plans Booth's ruin without any more compassion than a stone. Booth himself describes this kind of man to Amelia:

> All men, as well the best as the worse, act alike from the principle of self-love. Where benevolence therefore is the uppermost passion, self-love directs you to gratify it by doing good, and by relieving the distresses of others; for they are then in reality your own. But where ambition, avarice, pride, or any other passion governs the man and keeps his benevolence down, the miseries of all other men affect him no more than they would a stock or stone (X, 9).

In spite of Booth's ability to analyze the man ruled by passion, he never realizes the truth about James. Sherburn considers the failure to use Booth's disillusionment with James as a valuable opportunity overlooked for logical motivation in the progress toward conversion. [120]

It is during this first imprisonment also that Booth becomes involved with Miss Matthews. They too discuss the theory of the ruling passion; their subsequent behavior serves as an illustration of the ill effects of the false doctrine of moral irresponsibility. Miss Matthews agrees with every word she had read by "that charming fellow Mandevil"; Booth, Mandevillian though he is, repudiates this philosophy because Mandeville left out of his system the best passion, love, and attempted to derive the effects of that passion from the impulses of pride or fear (III, 4). The immediate response of Miss Matthews to the word <u>love</u> and the violation of morality in the name of love is part of the contrast between the physical passion she understands to be love and the kinship between love and goodness exemplified by Amelia. In the discussions and the actions of the first imprisonment, then, Fielding exhibits Booth's lack of a Christian belief and ethic as a guiding principle in life.

During the second imprisonment, this time for debts, Booth arrives at the next step in his spiritual progress. He is thrown into the company of a Stoic, who assures him that men can bear all of life's afflictions if they will but reason on the brevity of life and learn to place a just value on everything. Thus they can cure all eager wishes, abject fears, violent joy, grief—in short, all excesses of emotion. Fielding has Booth reject this philosophy, as he had fatalism. With the theory he agrees: Stoicism has utility in steeling the mind against misfortune. However, for Fielding, Stoicism fell short of the Christian doctrine of forgiveness for those who trespass against us and of consolation of divine love and heavenly bliss.[121] Booth argues that men may reason from their heads, as the Stoic advocates, but they act from their hearts (VIII, 10).

Booth's fortunes decline still further following the second imprisonment. His follies increase as his desperation grows: he loses heavily to Trent at gambling; then he loses all his money in the bribery attempt. His fortunes and his spiritual condition are at their lowest point. Even his advocates, and the advocates of Christian philosophy, reach a low point. Dr. Harrison is unable to interest an influential lord in Booth's favor without a more practical reason than merit (XI, 2), and events challenge even Amelia's faith in providence (XI, 9). In these dreary moments Booth shows how far he morally excels his brother officer Trent when he indignantly refuses to trade in his wife's virtue as a means of advancement, apparently the only means left. At this point Booth repudiates the practical application of his abstract theory that there are no absolutes of virtue. He recognizes the relationship between the goodness of the object of love and the concept of divine love, and this is a crucial step toward his final conversion.[122]

During the last imprisonment Booth, who has in turn rejected fatalism and Stoicism and has seen his own theory of the dominant passion lead from one calamity to a worse, is converted to Christianity by reading Dr. Barrow's sermons. Booth declares to Dr. Harrison, "I was never a rash disbeliever; my chief doubt was founded on this—that as men appeared to me to act chiefly from their passions their actions

could have neither merit nor demerit" (XII, 5). Dr. Harrison
answers for Fielding, that as men do act from their passions,
the Christian religion is useful and necessary in that it appeals
to the strongest of these passions, hope and fear.

Almost every commentator has found fault with Fielding's
handling of Booth's conversion as not adequately accounted for.
The conversion is more apparent to the reader than to Booth.
Dr. Harrison, the chief spokesman for orthodox Christian absolutes, makes his most convincing statements without Booth
present; so that while the clergyman may convince the reader,
he plays little part in the actual experience of Booth. Moreover, as previously noted, Dr. Harrison is not even aware that
Booth has been beset by doubts. Amelia, a firm believer in the
providence of God, is a more direct compelling force to virtue. However, she too plays little part in actively bringing
about Booth's progress toward conversion. The strongest
statement that she ever makes is the wish that Booth will talk
over his doubts with Dr. Harrison. For the most part, Booth's
conversion is a process of regeneration which he himself
achieves; his experience is in agreement with Christian belief
that salvation is necessarily individual. His conversion, however, is so fundamental to the moral scheme of the novel that
the reader feels the lack of a more forceful presentation involving Booth directly.

Booth rejoices to Dr. Harrison for what he calls "this last
instance of my shame," that is, the third imprisonment. This
reduction to an awareness of one's inadequacy and of complete
submission, is also, like the necessity for individual salvation,
an essential part of Christian experience. There is the obvious Christian symbolism in the use of three imprisonments,
reminiscent of Christ's imprisonment in the tomb and Paul's
three days of blindness. In the depth of his despair and shame,
Booth reads the sermons of Dr. Barrow in proof of the Christian religion, and all his doubts are removed. Once the basic
flaw of Booth's character is amended, the external distresses
are disposed of with speed. Hard on the heels of Booth's conversion comes the "death-bed" confession of Robinson, which
restores Amelia's inheritance (XII, 5,6). "Providence," de-

clares Dr. Harrison to the happy pair, "hath done you the justice at last which it will, one day or other, render to all men"
(XII, 7).

Objections to the rapidity with which that justice is done,
chiefly through the method of sudden revelation or discovery,
governed by forces totally outside the control of the main characters, are based on the assumption that the novel has as its
chief business the removal of external obstacles. It is the
same objection made to the ending of <u>Tom Jones</u> on the assumption that the chief concern is to remove the mystery of
Tom's birth, thus endowing him with the worldly requisites
for marriage. It is rather the central purpose of both novels
to bring their heroes to a state of moral maturity and spiritual
fitness. The external difficulties are critical, to be sure, but
once the moral issues are settled, they are brushed aside
without much regard for credibility. For Fielding, schooled
in the traditions of comic writing, the initiation, as well as the
denouement, of plot complications is a matter of easily arranged external circumstances. Blifil's villainy corresponds
to Betty's in the later novel. It is not by any blamable act of
either Tom or Booth that the difficulties begin. Whether in the
comedy of Tom Jones or in the serious preachments of <u>Amelia</u>,
what mattered to Fielding was the moral and spiritual condition of the hero. This being established as worthy, he removes
the obstacles and rewards his worthy characters. They are
now prepared and endowed for a serenely happy married life.

As in the earlier novels, Fielding uses the method of contrast to emphasize the desirable qualities of the ideal marriage. The chief target of much of his satire of marriage was
consistently the fashionable couple in high life. He routinely
establishes his ideal partners in a rural scene, away from the
corrupting forces of fashionable society. (The only exception
is <u>Jonathan Wild</u>, where Heartfree's trade as a merchant would
have made the change illogical.)

In <u>Amelia</u> the artificiality and meanness of city society are
painted in even darker shades than in the earlier works. The
couple which most graphically illustrates the fashionable marriage is the Jameses. The match is one of "love" for James,

that is, lust; it is one of prudence for Miss Bath, who gained everything by the bargain, including an unconcerned husband (IV, 4). Once James's appetite for her person is surfeited, he every day hates his wife more and more (V, 8). Mrs. James easily substitutes slavish devotion to fashionable life for love to a husband. Once elevated by her marriage, she is a somewhat less good-natured Charlotte (The Modern Husband) in her efforts to comply with the requirements of high life. Her conduct toward Amelia, as she alternates between her former self, the sympathetic and openhearted Miss Bath, and the new role of the fashionable Mrs. James, provides some of the best satire in the novel.

As a polite couple, the Jameses allow each other complete freedom. When Mrs. James offends her husband by interfering in his pleasures, however, he threatens to banish her to the country, the ultimate punishment for a fashionable lady. To avoid this calamity, Mrs. James agrees to serve as her husband's bawd in his effort to seduce Amelia, though she doubts his success with a woman whose virtue has the best guard in the world, "a most violent love for her husband" (XI, 1). The colonel and his lady "after living in a polite manner for many years together, at last agreed to live in a polite manner asunder" (XII, 9). Colonel James returns to his former mistress, Miss Mathews. Well provided for with an allowance from the colonel and an inheritance from her brother, Mrs. James divides her time among the heavens of the fashionable world—Tunbridge, Bath, and London—happily engaged nine of every twenty-four hours at cards.

A word should be added concerning Miss Matthews, whose whole career is an indictment of unrestrained passion. She never understands that love which is based on the goodness of the object rather than physical appetite. Though in the beginning she is the victim of Hebbers' design to marry her for her fortune, she provokes her own calamities by her vanity. Her behavior after she is deceived is of a piece with her early indiscretion.

As James was motivated by lust, Miss Bath by the advantages of a prudent marriage, and Miss Matthews by vanity,

Trent marries for revenge on his wife's father, who had cheated him of his inheritance. After the old man is ruined and he can hope for nothing from that quarter, Trent discovers that his wife has considerable commercial value. He accordingly serves as her agent in selling her to the peer; later the two operate an assembly, or as Fielding adds, more properly a bawdy-house, for the peer, who is omnipresent in the novel as a malignant force. The Trents, though more offensive than any other characters in the novel, are also victims of the corruption of high life.

The marriage between Mrs. Bennet and Sgt. Atkinson is of an entirely different character from the fashionable marriages. Mrs. Bennet is Fielding's most fully developed learned lady. [123] (See Appendix C.) Since he had a deep and abiding aversion for this type, she is the object of some sharp satire. It is written, however, in the "old" Fielding manner, ridicule tempered with tolerance. The duels of wit between Dr. Harrison and Mrs. Bennet provide some of the novel's rare moments of comedy; they are contests in which it is perhaps needless to add that the lady is reduced to absurdity (X, 1; 4). Actually she is a pretty good scholar, but Fielding meant to show that her classical learning was unnecessary, and possibly even detrimental, to a woman. Amelia's limited, but more practical, education in English plays and poetry, the divinity of Barrow, and the histories of Bishop Burnet (VI, 7) is more appropriate for the role of wife and mother.

Although Fielding ridicules Mrs. Bennet for her affectation of great understanding and adds the nice comic touch of having her somewhat fond of the bottle, he nevertheless portrays her sympathetically in a tragic early marriage. Her story is of interest for itself, but it also has relevance to Amelia's situation. Mrs. Bennet's experiences in many ways parallel Amelia's. She has, like Amelia, married for love and faced the woes of abject poverty. She endures even greater distress than Amelia in the deaths of her son and her husband. She is, like Amelia, the object of the designs of the malign peer, successful in her case. Mrs. Bennet is thus the means of saving Amelia from a similar fate and proves herself a steadfast

friend. In fact, the unifying theme in all of Mrs. Bennet's actions is a rather practical conception of the relation between
good and evil in human life which challenges Amelia's hermet-
ic kind of goodness. Mrs. Bennet struggles not so much to
exclude evil as to get the better of it. When she fails, her errors become a part of her armor in continuing the struggle.
The difference in the attitude of the two toward Mrs. Ellison,
once her true nature is clear to both, is evidence of the contrast between them. For Amelia, she is an evil creature to be
shunned; for Mrs. Bennet, she is someone to be put to good
use.[124]

There is a certain vanity in Mrs. Bennet, partly attribut-
able to her learning and her belief in her intellectual superiority, which contributes to her early disasters and which is lacking in Amelia. She continues to be willing to compromise her
virtue, or at least to endanger it, and Amelia's reputation as
well in order to get a commission for her new husband. The
resulting row between Amelia and Mrs. Bennet (now Mrs. Atkinson) is one of the liveliest scenes in the novel (X, 8).

It is against her false pride that Mrs. Bennet must fight and
triumph before she can propose marriage to Sgt. Atkinson,
who is her inferior socially. As Mrs. Atkinson, she is a fond
wife but, says Fielding, the sergeant is frequently "obliged to
pay proper homage to her superior understanding and knowledge" to keep peace in the family (XII, 9). He learns fairly
early in the marriage that there is but one way to subdue his
wife whenever her wrath is aroused, a strategy that brings
forth a tribute from the condescending wife: "Though you have
no learning, you have the best understanding of any man upon
earth" (X, 4). The reversal of the roles of husband and wife
as the dominant partner is exhibited as one likely to produce
an uncomfortable marriage. Nevertheless, Fielding allows
them, chiefly through the patient submission of Atkinson, a
prosperous and cheerful marriage blessed with two sons.

Against these marriages, all of which leave something to
be desired, the virtues of the ideal marriage are clear. They
are the qualities he extolled from the first to the last; the
statement is simply made more emphatic in Amelia. Rational

love, that is, goodness as the object of love, is its foundation.
Any marriage based on other motives—physical appetite, vanity, revenge, money—is a profanation of the holy purpose of
matrimony. Mutual trust is the source of harmony. Sufficient
means to support a family are essential. For the most perfect union, the wife is the subordinate partner, not learned in
areas superfluous to her role as the homemaker and instructress of her children. Religious conviction forms the guide
for the family.

If the assessment is correct that it is not Fielding's books
but the man himself that continues to win our admiration,[125]
then it is a certainty that <u>Amelia</u> is by far the most rewarding
of Fielding's novels. Fielding's presence overshadows his
characters, and it is Fielding for the most part without the
mask of the satirist. The success of the novel depends upon a
willingness to take it for what it is, a serious denunciation, as
Fielding himself said, "of glaring evils of the age." It cannot
in its totality be judged fairly on the basis of comparison with
<u>Tom Jones</u> or <u>Joseph Andrews</u> or <u>Jonathan Wild</u>. The remark-
able fact is that the views on marriage expressed in the last
novel are the generally sober statement of convictions hinted
at, or played upon in comic disguise, in all of the writing from
the beginning of his career to the end.

AFTERWORD

The progress of Henry Fielding from playwright to burlesque novelist to serious novelist is a story of movement from tolerant and genial acceptance of man as he is, an imperfect but improvable creature, in an imperfect but likewise improvable world, to a troubled, earnest anxiety for the harmony which existed as the center of his faith in order. He is perhaps the last great literary champion of the idea of orderliness in man's place in an ordered universe. Amelia is the rendering of that vision as a darkened one, threatened by loss of faith in the efficacy of the goodness of individuals. Billy Booth's ordeal reflects Fielding's own increasing despair. Booth cannot find his way out of his dilemma without faith; Fielding, one feels, is clinging with a kind of desperation to his own faith. The grim social picture of the last novel is his solemn warning that society will destroy itself on the larger plane, as it very nearly destroys the Booths on the smaller plane, without the harmony that grows out of responsible and benevolent actions motivating men. It is undoubtedly Fielding's most emphatic statement of Christian morality. The statement is clearly made throughout his work in the continuing pattern of his treatment of the subject of marriage.

It is tempting, if idle, to speculate whether Fielding, had he lived to produce other novels, might have gone the way of, say, Swift, toward complete pessimism. The fact is that in spite of the somber quality of Amelia, at the end of the novel, Fielding makes the leap of faith, as he had in all his novels, and leads his hero and heroine into a promised land of idealized happiness. Moreover, his last work, The Journal of a Voyage to Lisbon, the record of a dying man's final days, is notable for the survival of the qualities of compassion, patience, and amiability which mark Henry Fielding from the earliest record as a man of affirmative faith.

APPENDIX A. MARRIAGE LAW TO 1753

Except during the brief interval of Puritan rule, the laws governing marriage in England underwent no major change from the thirteenth century to 1753, the year of the passage of Lord Hardwicke's marriage act. The Restoration heritage of scorn of marriage is actually the culmination of a long tradition of disrepute in which the institution had existed. This contempt is not difficult to understand when one examines the evils arising from laws that were chaotic and inconsistent. One dominant theme running through the history of marriage law is the conflict between church and civil authorities for control, and most of the confusion can be traced to this struggle. A workable compromise between the two concepts was not to be effected until after Fielding's career as a novelist ended. The argument over the civil and sacramental bases of marriage appears in Jonathan Wild when the hermit attempts to dissuade Mrs. Heartfree from fidelity to her marriage vows on the grounds that marriage is no more than a civil policy (IV, 11).

From its earliest history in England, the Roman church had sought, in accord with its established policy, to incorporate marriage into its system of sacraments, thereby extending its realm to encompass all the important events of the individual's life from birth to death. In order to accomplish this goal in England, however, the church compromised its position by accepting many of the old Teutonic customs and attempting to adapt them to the doctrines of canon law. The legal inheritance from the Teutonic races was a civil contract of "bride sale." The lawful marriage was one in which the protectorship over the woman was purchased by the bridegroom from the woman's guardian. The steps were clearly formalized: first was the betrothal, involving payment by the bridegroom of the purchase

122

price for rights over the woman, and second, the actual nuptials.[126] The woman's rights as consort and yoke-fellow were also settled by contract. As early as the reign of Cnut (1016-1035), a woman was not forced to marry a man whom she disliked; however, marriage without a guardian's consent might entail loss of her inheritance.[127] Emphasis upon the right of the guardian to confer consent but not to force a marriage upon an unwilling child persisted through the centuries and receives much attention in Fielding's plays and novels. The right of a parent in choosing a child's marriage partner is debated in The Fathers. In Tom Jones the heart of Sophia's defense against Squire Western's proposal to marry her to Blifil is her willingness to grant her father the power to withhold his consent to any match which displeases him, but she insists on the same right. The squire's threats of disinheritance follow the tradition of the only legal recourse in dealing with an obstinate child. The coercion of a reluctant dependent with threats of disinheritance is also used in The Temple Beau. The binding nature of the parent's consent is evident in Amelia; Dr. Harrison declares that the mother cannot retract consent, once given, except for very serious cause.

The position of the church in superimposing its sacramental theory of marriage upon the Teutonic concept of a civil contract based on consent was inherently incongruous. Moreover, the church fostered a contradictory stand on the nature of marriage. As a sacrament marriage was a holy and mystic union, a view which directly opposed the teaching of the church that the celibate state was more glorious than the married. Most scholars of marriage law agree that the greatest harm was done to the development of healthy attitudes toward marriage by the church's emphasis upon St. Paul's famous text: "It is better to marry than to burn." The church might declare marriage to be a sacrament, but in practice it promoted the ideal that marriage was at best "a remedy for concupiscence. The generality of men and women must marry or they will do worse; therefore marriage must be made easy; but the very pure hold aloof from it as from a defilement."[128]

One of the most perplexing problems arising from efforts

to translate Teutonic customs into canon law was the question
of what constituted the actual marriage: the agreement between the bridegroom and the woman's guardian, the delivery
of the bride to the bridegroom, or the physical consummation
of the marriage. On the answer to this question depended such
important issues as the legitimacy of children and inheritance,
not to mention the happiness of the married pair. When by the
twelfth century the church had established its authority to leg-
islate such disputes, it seems to have abandoned common sense
in its recognition of two kinds of spousals: sponsalia per verba
de futuro, a promise between a man and woman that they will
in the future become husband and wife, such as made by Amelia and Billy Booth; and sponsalia per verba de praesenti, a
declaration between the two that they take each other as husband and wife at the moment of the declaration. The latter
was accepted without consummation as constituting a valid and
practically indissoluble marriage. Moreover, sponsalia per
verba de futuro, if followed by consummation, was accepted
as a valid marriage. By canon law after 1143, "a marriage
solemnly celebrated in church, a marriage of which a child
had been born, was set aside as null in favour of an earlier
marriage constituted by a mere exchange of consenting
words,"[129] whether followed by consummation or not. This
assumption that a marriage by words of consent before God
alone was more binding than a subsequent marriage according
to the laws of man and the church became the accepted interpretation until the Hardwicke act. It is obvious that difficulties
were to arise from such a nice distinction of grammar. As
Pollock and Maitland describe the pitfalls of such a system,
"Lovers are the least likely [of all human beings] to distinguish
between the present and the future tenses."[130] The disputes
before the church courts were filled with much swearing about
"I will" and "I do."

The binding nature of the promise de futuro is clear in
Amelia when Dr. Harrison insists that Mrs. Harris must
abide by her consent to Amelia's betrothal to Booth. Although
the de futuro vow did not legally constitute marriage unless
followed by consummation, the clergyman declares that the two

"ought as much to be esteemed man and wife as if the ceremony had already passed between [them]." Valid cause on the
part of one of the parties was necessary to cancel the vow. Dr.
Harrison attacks the suitor who seeks to come between Amelia
and Booth with the charge that he is "paying addresses to another man's wife." As a last resort, Dr. Harrison threatens
to join the two without the mother's approval, which she had
the right to refuse, not to retract (II, 5).

The church's recognition of the validity of such irregular
or clandestine marriages as were formed through these two
types of spousals did not constitute approval. There was indeed spiritual punishment of one sort or another, but usually
not very severe. Many respectable parties risked this punishment in order to have a private, but not a secret, ceremony to
avoid the expense of the public celebration which customarily
followed the rituals. The church encouraged the spouses to
seek the blessing of the church, thus assuring some measure
of publicity for the union and preventing marriages between
parties previously contracted.

By the end of the twelfth century or the early thirteenth, the
church had worked itself into approximately this position. It
approved a regular marriage based on consent of the parties
and conducted with publicity by the priest; it recognized irregular or clandestine marriage without approving it but leg-
islated in favor of a prior clandestine marriage over a regularly solemnized marriage within the church. These conditions existed with little change until the period of Puritan rule.

One might expect that marriage law would have undergone
radical change as a result of the Reformation in England, especially as the break with Rome was so closely allied to the
dispute over the validity of Henry VIII's "divorce" from Catherine and subsequent marriage to Anne. Such was not the
case. As Thomas Fuller declared in a sermon of 1643, "King
Henry the eight brake the Popes necke, but bruised not the
least finger of Popery ." The Reformation under Edward VI
was, like the reformer, a child. Mary's vigorous attempts to
arrest the progress of the Reformation were shortlived. And
"as for Queene Elizabeth," continues Fuller, "her Character

is given in that plaine, but true expression, that shee swept
the Church of England and left all the dust behind the door."[131]

In its practical results the Reformation had little effect on
law or theory as to the form of wedlock; with the nature of
marriage, the case was different. The dogma of its sacramental character was abandoned throughout the Protestant
world.[132] It was Martin Luther who, in his final stand on the
nature of marriage, provided the battle cry for abolition of
church control when he declared marriage to be a "temporal,
worldly thing" which does not concern the church.[133]

Puritan agitation in England for reform in marriage law
was part of the larger controversy over prelatical episcopacy,
a conflict which is fundamental to the history of the first half
of the seventeenth century. The first real blow to church control was struck when Parliament in 1642 abolished the temporal jurisdiction of the bishops. With the elimination of the
office of bishop in 1646 and the establishment of the new Puritan government in 1648, questions of marriage and divorce
were removed from the province of the church. Cromwell's
marriage act of 1653 was the triumph, of brief duration, of
civil over ecclesiastical control. Like many other reforms of
Cromwell's rule, the act was nullified upon the return to power
of the Stuarts. In their zeal to undo whatever had been initiated by Cromwell, the more vengeful Royalists even proposed
that all marriages performed under Cromwell's law should be
invalidated. Although this extreme proposal was not accepted,
the act of 1653 was superseded in practice by the laws in effect
before the Interregnum.

In the period between the Restoration and the passage of the
Hardwicke act, new abuses grew out of the anomalies of the
old system. One of the most spectacular of these was the
Fleet marriage, which resulted from the following set of circumstances. Before the reign of William (1689-1702), the
only punishment inflicted for secret marriages was spiritual.
However, in 1694 a tax, designed for providing additional rev-
enue rather than for controlling marriage, was imposed on all
marriages, varying in amount according to the rank of the

parties. The clergy were required to keep registers for the use of the tax collectors. A number of churches which had been exempt from the bishop's visitation claimed exemption likewise from this statute and thus developed a lucrative business in performing marriages without banns, license, or tax. The law was quickly amended to cover these churches and to punish any violations, but still a loophole existed. There were clergymen not included in the titles specified by the statute; these, often without benefices or definite habitation and often poor, were almost impossible to discover or convict. Moreover, some ministers, in prison for debt or other causes, married persons in prison, many unprincipled clergymen "resorting thither for the Purposes aforesaid, and in other Place for Lucre and Gain themselves."[134] Such an unprincipled clergyman is one of Booth's prison-mates. Though he does not perform any marriage service, his character is such that it is easy to believe him capable of violating any law.

To the Fleet prison came debtors from the entire kingdom, in such great numbers in fact that it was customary to allow those who could give security for their appearance upon summons to live in private lodging within the "rules of liberties" of the Fleet.[135] It was upon such condition that Booth was twice bailed after his arrest for debt.

Many disreputable clergymen set up shop in the precincts of the Fleet to take advantage of the traffic in matrimony, undaunted by threats of punishment. Howard describes the procedure in detail.[136] The marriage shop advertised, just as any ordinary business might, with signboards hung outside the place of business, hand-bills, journal notices of marriages performed with "everything conducted with the utmost decency and regularity." If such legitimate methods of advertising did not attract a satisfactory business, the Fleet marriage brokers employed plyers or touts to encourage trade by fair means or foul. One parson testified that on numerous occasions the couple to be married admitted to an acquaintance of no more than a week, a day, or less. Many taverns kept a Fleet parson in their employ as an extra accommodation for patrons. A contemporary writer describes a tavern party which ended with ten couples setting out for the Fleet as a joke. The joke took and the group returned two hours later wed. Questioned later about the incident, the tavern keeper could not recall the group because such marriage parties were common. Many instances of abductions, forced and fraudulent marriages by Fleet parsons add to the grimness of the record of abuses. The registers, required by law, were so falsified as to be useless as evidence. A single clergyman, between 1709 and 1740, the period of his confinement in the Fleet, performed 36,000 marriages.[137] The full import of Fielding's description of a bawd in The Wedding Day as having "sent more couples to bed without a license than any parson of the Fleet" (I, ii) was appreciated by his own audiences.

The Fleet marriages were performed by no means only between prisoners and the lower classes; many people of rank and wealth patronized these parsons because of the ease and privacy with which the ceremony could be performed. The expense was small, publicity was avoided, and parental consent for minors was ignored or sometimes forged.

There were other chapels—those of Savoy, St. James, the Duke's Palace, Holy Trinity Priory, and Mayfair[138]—which had a flourishing trade in marriages outside the law, but they never gained the notoriety of the Fleet.

Besides the irregularities of the Fleet and the other chapels, clandestine marriages, illegal but not invalid, were being performed again throughout the country. It was a case involving a clandestine marriage that became the cause célèbre which initiated the Hardwicke act.[139] The bill passed the House of Lords and, after a stormy controversy, the Commons, on June 6, 1753. Fielding is silent on this issue, which aroused such strong feeling that Hardwicke was burned in effigy. The Covent-Garden Journal was published during part of the time (1752) when the controversy was being hotly debated; but though he wrote on almost every other current topic, including several attacks on the laxity of the laws relating to adultery,[140] Fielding did not enter the fray over the marriage bill. His silence is the more unusual in view of his admiration for Lord Hardwicke, to whom he had dedicated his "Enquiry into the Causes of the Late Increase of Robbers," in January of 1751.[141] A possible explanation is the press of his duties as a magistrate at a time when his health was increasingly poor. As he notes in the Introduction of The Journal of a Voyage to Lisbon, he had suffered all through the year 1752 from "a lingering, imperfect gout," and was "fatigued to death."

In spite of the spirited opposition to the Hardwicke act, it was actually a moderate measure which served to stabilize marriage law. It provided that all marriages except those of Quakers, Jews, and members of the royal family[142] were to be performed only after the publication of banns or the obtaining of a license, during the canonical hours of eight to twelve noon, in an Anglican church or chapel by an Anglican clergyman with witnesses. Marriages solemnized in violation of the law except by special license of the archbishop were to be declared void and the offender was punishable by fourteen years' transportation. Falsification or destruction of the registers was punishable by death. Express consent of the guardian for minors was required for marriage by license; in the case of banns, silence was construed as consent.[143]

The Hardwicke act ends the relevant history of marriage law. Fielding's novels were all written before the date of the act. The pernicious practices against which the law was directed—distinction of types of spousals, clandestine marriage, abuses of the Fleet trade—were the legal background against which Fielding wrote.

APPENDIX B. DIVORCE LAW

Although the Hardwicke act stabilized marriage law, it made no provision for dissolution of marriage, a process as confused as was the contracting of marriage. There was, of course, no divorce in the modern sense, that is, dissolution of marriage with the right to remarry, before the granting of the first parliamentary divorce in 1698. Up to this date the chief means of release from an unhappy marriage alliance was by mutual consent to a separation, for example, the Fitzpatricks' agreement in Tom Jones and the Jameses' in Amelia.

This step required no legal procedures; the parties merely
agreed on the conditions of the separation and might, if recon-
ciled, resume the marriage. The alternative, an appeal to an
ecclesiastical court, was more complex. There were two
types of ecclesiastical decrees: <u>divortium a mensa et thoro</u>,
separation from bed and board, without the right of remar-
riage; and <u>divortium a vinculo matrimonii</u>, a declaration that
the marriage had been null from the beginning, any children
born during the union were bastards, and either party might
remarry. The former of these decrees was usually sought in
a case where one party would not agree to a separation by mutual consent. The church granted this separation as a temporary measure until reconciliation was effected, though such
reconciliation might indeed never occur. The chief causes for
ecclesiastical separation were cruelty and adultery. [144]

Since in theory a valid marriage was indissoluble, obviously
to obtain a nullification of marriage, the complainant must offer evidence of the invalidity of the marriage from the beginning. At least up to the accession of Elizabeth I there were
more grounds for annulment than for separation. [145] Corruption was so widespread among the clergy that during the medieval period almost anyone with money could have an impediment discovered in a disagreeable marriage. [146] The most
easily adapted impediments were those of forbidden degrees
of consanguinity, affinity, and spiritual relationship. [147] The
opportunities for discovering illegality were multiplied by
variations in interpreting the degrees. Within the prohibited
degrees distinctions were made; for example, kinship within
the sixth or seventh degree was cause for refusal to solemnize
a marriage but not a cause for nullifying one which had already
taken place. The impediments of affinity and spiritual relationship prohibited marriage between those who were related
by law or by participation in the same sacrament. A god-
mother or god-father was considered one in spirit with the
child and the family. "The doctrines of the church touching
affinity and relationship did not cease to perplex the courts,
molest the happiness of individuals and threaten the tranquility
of nations."[148]

Some improvement was effected by the time of Elizabeth I's accession; the grounds of annulment had been reduced to these:

1. Mutual consent in child marriages when the parties reached the age of consent. [149]
2. Pre-contract (the de futuro vow).
3. Bigamy.
4. Consanguinity within the degrees defined by law.
5. Impotence (during three years' cohabitation). [150]

Less frequent than separation and annulment was the suit for jactitation of marriage, which "denied the existence of the marriage contract or the marriage ceremony and requested the ecclesiastical court to silence forever the defendant who falsely claimed marriage."[151] This suit Alleman believes was probably used to evade the consequences of a clandestine marriage of which one party had tired, especially if the defendant could not prove the ceremony.

There was agitation during the years of the Puritan rule for reform in laws governing divorce, as the efforts of Milton testify. Little was achieved, however; Cromwell's act of 1653 made no specific mention of divorce except in granting authority to justices in cases of marriage of minors through fraud or abduction. Parliamentary divorce arose to give relief in those cases where no impediment could be established. The earliest of such decrees were grants of permission to remarry to prevent the extinction of specific peerages. [152] Of divorces in the modern sense, Alleman lists only six from 1698 to 1713.

Parliamentary divorce during the period under study was not frequent, the necessity for influence and/or wealth barring this avenue to most. No provision for divorce was included in the Hardwicke act of 1753. The brightest hope of escape from an unsatisfactory marriage remained separation or nullification on the basis of impediments. Although, according to Alleman, many of the abuses had been eliminated by the time of Elizabeth's reign, such an intricate system made it easy to stretch the law. That it was still being stretched more than a century after Elizabeth is evident in Fielding's first play in

1728. Fielding has Sir Positive Trap assure his niece, who
pleads pre-contract to avoid an arranged marriage, "The law
dissolves all contracts without a valuable consideration; or, if
it did not, a valuable consideration would dissolve the law"
(LISM, II, vii).

On first consideration, it is somewhat surprising that Fielding, who studied the law after he abandoned his career in the
theatre, made so little use of the many irregularities of the
law. The material lent itself easily to comic treatment; moreover, extensive use had been made during the Restoration
period proper of matrimonial law as material for comedy.
Many a plot denouement was based on a loophole in the law. In
Fielding's plays there are occasional references to pre-contract, mock marriage (LISM), clandestine marriage and forced
marriage (TB); however, the situations are never developed
and never serve as the solution to plot complication. Practically nothing appears in the novels of such irregularities. This
slight use of the technicalities of the law is not so surprising,
however, when one remembers that Fielding was interested in
the human problem rather than the niceties of law. He attempts to lead men into a better life by reliance on and practice of fundamental Christian doctrine, in marriage as in other relationships. The law will be more just when men are
more just, not the other way around. He is concerned in the
plays and novels with people rather than the law for itself and
with popular attitudes and practices. The confusion of the law
itself—at best poorly conceived, inconsistent in theory and
practice up to 1753, and inefficiently administered—promoted
the popular contempt for marriage, which was clearly as precarious an undertaking in legal terms as it was in human
terms. It is in human terms that Fielding and the greatest of
his contemporaries dealt.

APPENDIX C. POPULAR ATTITUDES TOWARD MARRIAGE
AND WOMEN

Addison declared in 1711 that nothing marked the times as
a degenerate and vicious age more than the common ridicule

which passed on marriage (Spectator, No. 261, Dec. 29, 1711).
He was criticizing the continuation in his own century of cynical attitudes which have a long tradition. His own satirical
account of a young woman of fashion's advice to a recently
married friend is typical of this cynicism:

> After six months of marriage to hear thee talk of love...
> is a little extravagant.... Pray thee leave these whim-
> sies, and come to town and live and talk like other mor-
> tals.... I am so afraid you will make so silly a figure as
> a fond wife, that I cannot help warning you not to appear
> in any public places with your husband, and never to
> saunter about St. James's park together: if you presume
> to enter the ring at Hyde-park together you are ruined
> forever; nor must you take the least notice of one another,
> at the playhouse, or opera, unless you would be laughed
> at.... I would recommend the example of an acquaint-
> ance of ours to your imitation; she is the most negligent
> and fashionable wife in the world; she is hardly ever
> seen in the same place with her husband, and if they hap-
> pen to meet, you would think them perfect strangers; she
> was never heard to name him in his absence, and takes
> care he shall never be the subject of any discourse that
> she has a share in.
>   (Spectator, No. 254, Dec. 21, 1711)

Perhaps more than a fair share of the blame for contempt
of marriage was laid at the door of women, who were usually
portrayed as vain and frivolous creatures. Inextricably involved in the attitudes toward marriage was the low estimate
of women. The church here, as in its interpretation of marriage, played a major and a paradoxical role. Just as the
church had proclaimed marriage to be a sacred and mystic
union but had at the same time regarded it as a necessary evil
to be entered into only for propagation of the race and as a
preventive measure against sexual promiscuity, always glor-
ifying the single state as the higher way of life, it took a contradictory stand in its attitude toward woman. On the one hand,

it elevated the worship of Mary almost to the level of worship
of Christ; on the other hand, it took a dim view indeed of the
nature of the ordinary woman. St. Chrysostom (345?-407)
catalogs her as a "necessary evil, a natural temptation, a desirable calamity, a domestic peril, a deadly fascination and a
painted ill."[153]

Although woman had occupied an inferior social position
long before the establishment of Christianity, emphasis upon
her supposed moral inferiority to man was a peculiar contri-
bution of the church fathers. At best, so the reasoning went,
she was a second step from divinity in her creation from Adam
rather than from divine materials; and it was Eve who was
first deceived, sinned, and led man into evil.

Just how seriously the church considered the woman's
moral inferiority is brought home to the modern student by the
fact that a debate in the church councils of one thousand years'
duration on the question of whether woman possessed a soul
was not settled in the affirmative until the sixteenth century.[154] That woman's moral status in the eyes of the ecclesiastics was not far exalted even as late as the sixteenth
century above what it had been in St. Chrysostom's day can be
seen in Bishop Aylmer's description in a sermon delivered,
interestingly enough, before Queen Elizabeth:

Women are of two sorts, some of them are wiser, better
learned, discreeter, and more constant than a number of
men; but another and a worse sort of them, and the most
part, are fond, foolish, wanton flibbergibs, tatlers, trif-
lers, wavering, witless, without council, feeble, careless, rash, proud, dainty, nice, tale-bearers, eaves-
droppers, rumour-raisers, evil-tongued, worse-mind-
ed, and in every way doltified with the dregs of the devil's dunghill.[155]

Little change in tone can be detected in the abbreviated summary of woman's faults by another distinguished churchman,
of the eighteenth century: the generality of women, said Dean

Swift, are "fools, prudes, coquettes, gamesters, saunterers, endless talkers of nonsense, splenetic idlers, intriguers, given to scandal and censure."[156] It should be added in fairness to Swift—and women—that he attributed the shortcomings to neglect of their education, in which he had a life-long interest, and he was not a great deal kinder in his comments about the young men of his day.

Women fared little better through the ages at the hands of literary men than they had at the hands of the ecclesiastics. While the latter excoriated them for moral weakness, the former delighted in satirizing them for their foibles and follies. By the Middle Ages there was a well-established tradition of the vain, frivolous, willful creature; no better example exists than Chaucer's immortal Alice of Bath. It is impossible to trace this tradition in detail here, but for evidence that it flourished in the seventeenth century, only a cursory examination of Restoration drama is necessary. In the eighteenth century Pope echoes the primary characteristics of Alice in these typical barbed lines in "Of the Characters of Women":

In men, we various ruling passions find;
In women, two almost divide the kind;
Those, only fixed, they first or last obey,
The love of pleasure and the love of sway.

Even Addison, sympathetic toward women and favorable toward reform of their education, could not resist the impulse to satirize them in the Guardian when he offered as one good reason for educating them that since they had a "plenty of words, it is a pity they should not put... [them] to use. If the female tongue will be in motion, why should it not be set to go right?" (No. 155, Sept. 8, 1713).

There are noble portraits of women throughout English literature, from Anglo-Saxon times to the period of this study; however, much that was commendatory fell into such rigidly categorized types as saints' lives, Mary poems, and romances. In the latter, even those ladies whose conduct was exemplary were usually no more than motivating devices for the adventures of chivalrous knights. The most notable exceptions to these generalizations are the creations of the Renaissance writers. Women in general fared better during this period than in the subsequent era, partly because of the influence of powerful women rulers like Elizabeth, perhaps in some measure because of the unusual number of accomplished women of the period (Sir Thomas More's daughter, Lady Jane Grey, Queen Mary and Elizabeth herself), and partly because of the influence of the Italian cult of exaggerated courtesy. The latter tradition, inherited by the Elizabethan sonneteers, even if only as a literary fashion, glorified woman "as the sum of all perfections and the inspiration of every virtue."[157] Certainly the reputation of women sank in the period which followed. This reversal may be accounted for by the licentiousness of the Caroline courts, which gave notoriety to a number of spectacular women, and by the Puritan emphasis on woman as a snare and a delusion. Powell argues that

> the ecclesiastical recognition among Protestant sects of the possibility of woman's occupying a higher position in matrimonial society than that of a mere instrument for carnal desires, is important in marking the beginning of the end of the degradation [of women by the church].[158]

That both these contradictory views could exist in the mind of a single man is eloquently testified to by the dilemma of John Milton, who aspired to a marriage which was a "union of hearts" providing "enrichment...in all the charities of the family,"[159] but who made the painful discovery that love and marriage have alike the power to mar or to make a man's life. The result is the extremes of the idealized apostrophe to wedded love in Paradise Lost and the denunciation of Eve, and the race of women, as the "fair defect of nature."

At the opening of the eighteenth century, woman was still the object of suspicion and concern to the ecclesiastics for moral weakness; of pure invective to those with private grievances; and often of satire to the witty secular writers. When one attempts to determine from contemporary documents just what the position of women was and the popular idea of their character, it is necessary, as Powell cautions, "to accept only cum magno grano salis the testimony of all who have any axe to grind, be it sentimental, religious, or otherwise."[160] Perhaps the most trustworthy picture of what a woman's status was, and the glimmerings of progress toward a place in her own right, can be found in the proposals of those who wished to guide her education and conduct.

The recurring theme of the programs of education for women and advice on conduct is the preparation of the young woman as a convenience for man: she is admonished constantly to be a good daughter, wife, and mother. By good is meant submissive, obedient, and virtuous. She is warned to confine herself to acquiring only that knowledge which will contribute to the fulfillment of her proper role. Concerning education for her own satisfaction, little is said. Consequently, the liberal view expressed by Defoe in An Essay on Projects (1698) is all the more remarkable. He is far ahead of the numerous reformers who spoke out in the early years of the eighteenth century, as much in the liberality of his proposals as in time. He denounces what he calls the barbarous denial of the advantages of learning to women. Their being "conversible at all" was the wonder, with the limitation of their instruction to stitching, sewing, or making baubles and reading and writing to the extent only of signing their names.[161]

"What has the woman done," he asks, "to forfeit the privilege of being taught?.... Shall we upbraid women with folly, when 'tis only the error of this inhuman custom that hindered them being made wiser?" He insists that the words weakness of women would be lost if the women's souls were refined and improved by teaching. Practical man that he was, Defoe wisely appealed to the self-interest of those who governed the education of women rather than to the principle of right. It would be to the advantage of men to provide for the improvement of the girls who were to be their wives, to assure themselves of more suitable and serviceable mates.

Bless us! What care do we take to breed up a good horse and to break him well, and what a value we put upon him when it is done, and all because he should be fit for our use; and why not a woman? Since all her ornaments and beauty, without suitable behavior, is a cheat in nature.

Beyond usefulness, he declares, there is the final reward of delight, for "a woman of sense and manners is the finest and most delicate part of God's creation; the glory of her Maker ...his darling creature."[162]

The inadequacy of the typical training of young girls is the subject of attack in Spectator No. 66.

When a girl is safely brought from her nurse before she is capable of forming one single notion... she is delivered to the hands of her dancing master... and is taught a fantastical gravity of behavior and forced to a particular way of holding her head, heaving her breast, and moving with her whole body; and all this under pain of never having a husband.... This gives the young lady wonderful workings of the imagination, what is to pass between her and this husband, that she is every moment told of, and for whom she seems to be educated.

In Spectator No. 10, Addison describes the indolence encouraged in women.

The toilet is their great scene of business, and the right adjusting of their hair the principal employment of their lives. The sorting of a suit of ribbons is reckoned a very good morning's work; and if they make an excursion to a mercer's or a toyshop, so great a fatigue makes them unfit for anything else all the day after. Their more serious occupations are sewing and embroidery, and their drudgery the preparations of jellies and sweetmeats.

Surely, he adds, there must be some middle course between her present state, with too much emphasis upon her person and frivolous activities on one hand, and too much indulgence in

study on the other—so that the "mind and body [may] improve
together." In many families of his acquaintance, "all the girls
hear of, in this life, is, that it is time to rise and come to
dinner, as if they were...wholly provided for when they are
fed and clothed" (Tatler No. 248, Nov. 9, 1710). The common
design of parents is to get their girls off as well as they can;
and, he laments, they make no conscience of putting into the
future husband's hands "a bargain for our whole life, which
will make our hearts ache every day of it" (Tatler, No. 248,
Nov. 9, 1710).

The echo of the theme of education of woman for the convenience of her husband is everywhere heard in the Spectator,
the Tatler, and the Guardian, and in most of the writing on the
subject elsewhere. Only such authors were recommended by
Addison, Steele, and other contributors to their papers

> as do not corrupt while they divert, but tend...to im-
> prove them as they are women.... They shall all tend to
> advance the value of their innocence as virgins, improve
> their understanding as wives, and regulate their tender-
> ness as parents. (Italics mine)

The desired result of this program will be knowledge that appears only as cultivated innocence. No better statement of the
ideal of the eighteenth century for education of women could be
found.

"Learning and knowledge are perfections in us, not as we
are men, but as we are reasonable creatures," Addison declares in Guardian No. 155. Nevertheless, not too much
learning and knowledge are recommended in the case of wom-
en; he adds in a subsequent paper that "it is indeed an unhappy
circumstance in a family, where the wife has more knowledge
than the husband," though better this evil than no one in the
family with sense (Guardian No. 165, Sept. 19, 1713).

No greater abomination existed than the "learned lady," the
special target of writers throughout the eighteenth century.
The exact point at which enough learning ceased and too much

began—Addison's desired middle course—was difficult to fix.
Louis B. Wright maintains that the literacy of women as early
as the Renaissance has been underestimated.[163] The accom-
plishments of some remarkable Renaissance women have been
generally acknowledged; but Wright contends that some rudi-
mentary education for women was widespread. Such advocates
of educating women as Richard Mulcaster (1581), Thomas Sal-
ter (1574), and Edward Hake (1574) emphasize training for religious purposes, with a caution against "amorous books,vaine
stories and fond trifeling fancies."[164] With the spread of Pur-
itanism, the impetus increased for women to master at least
skills of reading sufficient to enable them to fulfill their obligation for the moral instruction of their families. Although
the great criterion both for teaching and for the substance to
be taught was one of moral utility,numerous contemporary al-
lusions indicate that romances were as popular with middle
and lower class women in the early seventeenth century as
with their more aristocratic sisters. The feminine audience
had reached such proportions by the last quarter of the sixteenth century that authors were beginning to cater to women,
whether aristocratic ladies or tradesmen's wives.[165] A wide
audience was in the making for a Pamela, with its romantic
episodes clothed in the guise of moral instruction.

Few writers of the eighteenth century,even of the extreme-
ly conservative group, would have quarreled with the tradition
of teaching women the rudiments of education. However, study
beyond what they considered the native capabilities, or limitations, came in for satire. The learned lady had been subjected to satiric portrayal as early as the Renaissance,[166] but the
sting grows sharper in the late seventeenth and early eighteenth century. Swift advises a recently married young friend
to cultivate her mind in order to gain and preserve the esteem
of her husband,for endowments of the mind will make her person more agreeable to him. But she should not ape "those
learned women who have lost all Manner of Credit by their
impertinent Talkativeness and Conceit of themselves."[167]
Fielding was in complete agreement with this sentiment and

created notable caricatures of the type in Bridget Allworthy and Mrs. Western in Tom Jones and in Mrs. Bennet in Amelia. Myra Reynolds believes that Fielding satirized Mrs. Western only because her pretensions to learning were unjustified and insists, on the basis of opinions which he expressed in the prefaces to his sister's novels, that for a modest woman of real learning and ability he had great respect.[168] The fact remains that in his own fiction he created no such modest woman of learning.

One may object with justification to assuming Fielding's dislike of the learned lady on the evidence of such declarations as Squire Western's to his sister that "petticoats should not meddle" in subjects that are the province of men; Squire Western is not a character whose opinions can be equated with Fielding's. Allworthy and Dr. Harrison do frequently serve as mouthpieces for the author. Allworthy expresses his contempt for the breed of aggressive lady scholars when he judges Sophia's greatest charm to be her lack of pretense to wit or to that wisdom which results only from great learning and experience (XVII, 3). Dr. Harrison's attack on Mrs. Bennet is the sharpest Fielding wrote on this subject; the usually charitable clergyman, quoting from Homer, tells her: "Go home and mind your business. Follow your spinning, and keep your maids to their work" (X, 4). The frequency of Fielding's satire at the expense of the learned lady and the glorification of women like Sophia and Amelia who have no claim to learning seem to indicate conclusively that Fielding shared the opinion of his contemporaries toward too much learning for women.

The authors cited—Addison, Steele, Defoe, Swift, Fielding—are, though in varying degrees, the more generous spirits, by no means typical. Much more usual is the advice given to a young lady to accept her lot in life as "the weaker vessel" and to strive to serve her husband's will. One father's very practical advice to a daughter whom he fears he has sheltered too much can be summed up as "Take what you get and make the best of it." She must be reasonable and agreeable so long as her husband treats her tolerably. If it is her fate to get a husband given to drunkenness, infidelity, sullenness, or stingi-

ness, then her amiability will make things better for both. If
he is an absolute brute, her only recourse is to leave him and
live in seclusion; such were the realities of the situation.[169]

Steele's tribute to his wife in the dedication to Volume III of
The Ladies Library summarizes the qualities of the ideal woman: The tender mother,/ The fond wife,/ The prudent mistress,/ The frugal housekeeper,/ The cheerful companion,/
The happy slave to/ Her powerful husband.[170] A woman was
perhaps not literally a slave to a powerful husband, as she has
found ways and means of prevailing ever since Eve, but legally
she had no status apart from her husband's or her father's.
Her education was limited. Whenever she deviated from the
accepted ideal, she was denounced by the moralists or ridiculed by the satirists. Nevertheless, from the earliest years
of the eighteenth century, the condition of women gradually
changed, with her emergence as a being of worth, of and for
herself. The change was indeed gradual. The best evidence
that it was occurring is the intensity of the debate over her nature, her education, and her proper role as she entered new
fields of public life such as authorship and the theatre and pursued education for her own satisfaction.

Brief mention should be made of the influence of Samuel
Richardson, whose part as the immediate stimulus to Fielding's career as a novelist is discussed in Chapter III. It would
be difficult to overstate the impact of his anatomizing of the
deepest feelings of his women characters. However the more
acute readers might suspect Pamela's motives, she became a
symbol of the morally superior woman; and more significant
still to the cause of women was Clarissa Harlowe, who, although a woman of her age in many respects, is chiefly com-
mendable because of her loyalty to herself. The vogue of
Clarissa was never so great as that of Pamela, but the moral
superiority of the later character is unquestioned. Fielding's
reaction to the two suggests this superiority; after his devastating attacks on the shoddy virtue of Pamela in both Shamela
and Joseph Andrews, he generously praised the characterization of Clarissa (The Jacobite's Journal, January 2, 1747-48).

Fielding provides as great variety in his portrayal of women as he does in his general characterization of marriage. As a playwright he filled the stage with the butterfly women common to Restoration literature and as a mature novelist never ceased to ridicule affectation in women; but the idealized marriage portrayed in his work is always centered on the virtue and moral strength of a beautiful woman, a Sophia or an Amelia.

NOTES

Introduction
1. Gellert Spencer Alleman, Matrimonial Law and the Materials of Restoration Comedy (Wallingford, Pa., 1942), p. 5.

Chapter 1
2. The case is recorded in the Registry Book of Lyme Regis, Nov. 12, 1725. Cited by Wilbur L. Cross, The History of Henry Fielding (New York, 1963), I, 51. Cross's is the most complete biography of Fielding.
3. Mary P. Willcocks, A True Born Englishman (London, 1947), p. 26.
4. Cross, I, 53-54.
5. Ibid., I, 169.
6. Ibid., I, 172.
7. Ibid., II, 62.

Chapter 2
8. The number varies because of Fielding's collaboration with other playwrights. This figure is based on the edition of Leslie Stephen, The Works of Henry Fielding, VIII-X (London, 1882). There is no complete study of the plays of Fielding. The most detailed and comprehensive accounts of his dramatic career have been made by his biographers, who concern themselves primarily to place the plays in a biographical context. Historians of the drama stress the relationship of Fielding's plays to the theatre of the period. Special studies of individual plays generally seek sources in contemporary life, with particular attention to their political background.
9. John H. Smith, The Gay Couple (Cambridge, Mass., 1948), pp. 224-226.

10. Charles B. Woods, "Notes on Three of Fielding's Plays," PMLA, LII (1937), 367.
11. Joseph Wood Krutch, Comedy and Conscience after the Restoration (New York, 1949), p. 5.
12. John Loftis (Comedy and Society from Congreve to Fielding; Stanford, Calif., 1959) traces the gradual evolution of the merchant as a respected character in sentimental drama as a part of the triumph of the emerging middle class. Fielding usually follows the older pattern of the merchant as the object of ridicule.
13. Smith, p. 77.
14. Ibid., p. 194.
15. Ibid., p. 199.
16. P. F. Vernon, "Marriage of Convenience and the Moral Code of Restoration Comedy," Essays in Criticism, XII (October, 1962), 375.
17. Austin Dobson, Fielding (New York, 1883), p. 18.
18. Cross, I, 118-119.
19. Woods, pp. 362-367.

Chapter 3
20. Ernest A. Baker, The History of the English Novel (London, 1930), IV, 28.
21. Ian Watt, The Rise of the Novel (Berkeley, 1957), Chapter 5, especially pp. 127-144.
22. Robert P. Utter and Gwendolyn Needham, Pamela's Daughters (New York, 1937), pp. 20-21.
23. Ibid., pp. 31-33.
24. Watt, p. 157.
25. Utter and Needham, p. 31.
26. A. R. Wagner, English Ancestry (London, 1961), pp. 84-101.
27. William M. Sale, Jr. "From Pamela to Clarissa," The Age of Johnson (New Haven, 1949), pp. 129-131.
28. Watt, pp. 161, 155; see Michael D. Bell, "Pamela's Wedding and the Marriage of the Lamb," PQ, XLIV (1970), 100-112.
29. Baker, IV, 28.
30. Family name, transmitted through male lines is of course a factor. See Wagner, pp. 95-96, on this point.

31. Bernard Kreissman, Pamela-Shamela (University of Nebraska
     Studies, n.s. No. 22; Lincoln, May, 1960), p. 15.

32. This apt phrase is Martin Battestin's, in Joseph Andrews and
     Shamela (Boston, 1961), p. xvi—hereafter cited as Battestin,
     Joseph Andrews and Shamela.

33. F. Homes Dudden, Henry Fielding, His Life, Works, and
     Times (Oxford, 1952), I, 314.

34. Martin C. Battestin, The Moral Basis of Fielding's Art
     (Middletown, Conn., 1959), p. 8—hereafter cited as Battestin,
     Fielding's Art.

35. Baker, IV, 93.

36. Dobson, p. 73.

37. Kreissman, p. 20.

38. Maurice Johnson, Fielding's Art of Fiction (Philadelphia, 1961),
     pp. 50-51.

39. Battestin, Joseph Andrews and Shamela, p. xxxi.

40. Battestin, Fielding's Art, p. 114.

41. Dick Taylor, Jr., "Joseph as the Hero of Joseph Andrews,"
     Tulane Studies, 1957, VII, 91. This study gives the fullest ac-
     count of the emergence of Joseph as a serious hero.

42. Battestin, Joseph Andrews and Shamela, p. xxxi.

43. Kreissman, p. 21.

44. Ibid., pp. 21-22.

45. Dudden, I, 336.

46. Ibid., I, 352.

47. Battestin, Joseph Andrews and Shamela, p. xxxviii.

48. Arnold Kettle, An Introduction to the English Novel
     Hutchinson's University Library, 1951), I, 75-76.

49. Dudden, I, 480-483 summarizes the evidence for all the theses
     on date of composition.

50. Aurelien Digéon, Le Texte de Romans de Fielding (Paris, 1923),
     pp. 9-58, catalogs the textual changes in the two editions.

51. Henry Fielding, Miscellanies, ed. Leslie Stephen, Works
     (London, 1882), VII, 320-321.

52. William R. Irwin, The Making of Jonathan Wild (New York,
     1941), pp. 92-93.

53. Cross, I, 422-423; Baker, IV, 109, n. 2; and others suggest
     that Fielding's fabrication of a genealogy for Wild was a

travesty of William Musgrave's genealogical tree in The Brief
and True History of Robert Walpole and his Family, which
devotes thirty-eight of its seventy-eight pages to Walpole's
ancestry.

54. Kathleen Lynch, The Social Mode of Restoration Comedy (New
York, 1926) cites in detail the plays which use this device:
pp. 83-83, 146, 162, 201-203.

55. Henry Fielding, The Covent-Garden Journal, ed. Gerard E.
Jensen (New Haven, 1915), I, 178-180—hereafter cited as
Covent-Garden Journal.

56. The 1743 edition included a chapter heading: "A very wonderful chapter indeed, which to those who have not read many
voyages, may seem incredible...." Digéon, pp. 53-58, gives
the 1743 version and comments on the changes.

57. Irwin, p. 99.

Chapter 4

58. Watt, pp. 269-270.

59. George Sherburn, "Fielding's Social Outlook," PQ, XXXV
(January, 1956), 8.

60. Ibid., p. 2.

61. A forceful parallel to this philosophy is found throughout the
novels of Jane Austen, who thought it was wrong to marry for
money, but silly to marry without it. In Persuasion she presents the conflict between two schemes of values: those of
prudence and those of love. Though ten years of unhappiness
result from the heroine's choice, she remains committed to
prudential values. (Andrew H. Wright, Jane Austen's Novels,
New York, 1954, p. 161).

62. Watt, p. 281. For a full account of the reception of the novel,
charges and defenses, see Frederic T. Blanchard, Fielding
the Novelist (New Haven, 1927), pp. 26-78.

63. Baker, IV, 152.

64. Watt, p. 283.

65. Baker, IV, 130. See also Alan D. McKillop, Samuel Richardson, Printer and Novelist, p. 173, for Richardson's complaint
against making Tom a "kept fellow" in an age when "keeping is
become a fashion."

66. Dudden, II, 623.

67. "Henry Fielding," Times Literary Supplement, LIII (October 8, 1954), 641.
68. J. Middleton Murry, "In Defense of Fielding," Unprofessional Essays (London, 1956), pp. 13-14.
69. William Empson, "Tom Jones," Kenyon Review, XX (Spring, 1958), 237.
70. Ibid., p. 218.
71. Watt, p. 283.
72. Blanchard, pp. 40-41.
73. McKillop, p. 173.
74. Dobson, p. 124.
75. Utter and Needham, p. 373.
76. Ibid., pp. 155-156.
77. Watt, p. 274.
78. George Sherburn, "Fielding's Amelia: An Interpretation," ELH, III (March, 1936), p. 9.
79. Watt, p. 284.

Chapter 5
80. Monthly Review, December, 1751, quoted in Blanchard, p. 80.
81. Henry Fielding, Amelia, ed. George Saintsbury (London, 1939), p. x—hereafter cited as Saintsbury, Amelia.
82. Baker, IV, 155.
83. C. J. Rawson, "Nature's Dance of Death," Eighteenth Century Studies, Part II (Summer, 1970), #4, IV, 507.
84. Sherburn, "Fielding's Amelia," p. 1.
85. Covent-Garden Journal, I, 178-180; 186-187.
86. Blanchard, pp. 79-103.
87. Covent-Garden Journal, I, 65.
88. Blanchard, p. 81.
89. McKillop, Samuel Richardson, p. 175.
90. Blanchard, pp. 98-99. Richardson's condemnation was based, so he says, on the reading of the first two chapters.
91. Covent-Garden Journal, I, 179.
92. There are still divergent views. William M. Sale, Jr., for example, states that "Richardson's successors—Fielding and Smollett—failed to create a successful female character." Samuel Richardson, Pamela (New York, 1958), p. vi.

93. Sherburn, "Social Outlook," p. 13.
94. James A. Work, "Henry Fielding, Christian Censor," The
     Age of Johnson (New Haven, 1949), p. 147.
95. Sherburn, "Social Outlook," p. 14. Sherburn had recognized
     the dual problem in his earlier "Fielding's Amelia: An Inter-
     pretation," though not in these precise terms.
96. Gerard E. Jensen, "Fashionable Society in Fielding's Time,"
     PMLA, XXXI (1916), 79.
97. Augustus R. Towers, "Amelia and the State of Matrimony,"
     Review of English Studies, n. s. V (1954), p. 155.
98. In the year following the publication of Amelia Fielding wrote
     on this subject in the Covent-Garden Journal, Nos. 25, 50, 67,
     and 68.
99. Baker, IV, 163.
100. Ibid. , IV, 159.
101. Saintsbury summarizes these critical estimates in Amelia,
     pp. vii-ix.
102. For opposing views, contrast Banerji, p. 229 and Baker, IV,
     189, with Sherburn, "Social Outlook," p. 21.
103. F. R. Leavis, The Great Tradition (New York, 1948), p. 4.
104. Murry, pp. 38-46 gives a spirited answer to Leavis.
105. Covent-Garden Journal, I, 178-179.
106. Utter and Needham, pp. 158-159.
107. Towers, p. 145.
108. Ibid. , p. 156.
109. Saintsbury, Amelia, p. ix.
110. Baker, IV, 159.
111. Sherburn, "Social Outlook," p. 14.
112. Towers, p. 156.
113. Digéon, Novels, p. 206.
114. Baker, IV, 167.
115. Banerji, p. 236.
116. Sherburn, "Fielding's Amelia," p. 5.
117. Alan Wendt, "The Naked Virtue of Amelia," ELH, XXVII (1960),
     p. 138.
118. Work, p. 140.
119. The Loeb Classical Library Translation by Platnauer, quoted
     by Sherburn, "Fielding's Amelia," p. 6.

120. Sherburn, "Fielding's Amelia," p. 9.
121. Work, p. 141.
122. Wendt, pp. 142-143.
123. An especially full discussion of Mrs. Bennet is given in John
     S. Coolidge's "Fielding and 'Conservation of Character,'"
     Modern Philology, LVII (May, 1960), 253-258. Says Coolidge,
     "It hardly seems too much to say that Mrs. Atkinson saves the
     novel" (p. 258).
124. Ibid., pp. 257-258.
125. Sale, p. 133.

Appendix
126. George E. Howard, A History of Matrimonial Institutions
     (Chicago, 1904), I, 258-259.
127. Sir Frederick Pollock and Frederic W. Maitland, The History
     of English Law before the Time of Edward I, 2nd ed.
     (Cambridge, 1911), II, 364-365.
128. Ibid., II, 385.
129. Ibid., II, 367.
130. Ibid., II, 369.
131. Quoted in Chilton Latham Powell, English Domestic Relations,
     1487-1653 (New York, 1917), p. 28.
132. Howard, I, 386.
133. Ibid., I, 388.
134. Ibid., I, 437.
135. "The rules of liberties of this [the Fleet] comprehend all
     Ludgate-Hill to the Old Bailey on the north side, and to the
     Cock-alley on the south; both sides of the Old Bailey to Fleet-
     lane; all Fleet-lane and the east side of the market, from
     Fleet-lane to Ludgate Hill."—Harrison, New and Universal
     History of London, II, 447, quoted by Howard I, 437, n. 3.
136. Ibid., I, 438-444.
137. Ibid., I, 440. A Mayfair clergyman performed an average of
     six thousand marriages a year. A nearby church solemnized
     only fifty regular marriage contracts in a year (p. 443).
138. Rosamond Bayne-Powell, Eighteenth-Century London Life
     (London, 1937), p. 53.
139. The Cochrane vs. Campbell case, Howard, I, 448.
140. Covent-Garden Journal, Nos. 25, 50, 67, and 68.

141. Cross, II, 255.
142. Royal marriages had always been excepted from the laws governing marriage for the public.
143. Howard, I, 458-459.
144. Alleman, p. 112.
145. Powell, p. 8.
146. Alleman, p. 125.
147. For a complete list of impediments, see Powell, pp. 72-74. n. 2.
148. Howard, I, 353. The most famous case in English history of affinity "threatening the tranquility of nations" is Henry VIII's actions against Catherine, his deceased brother's wife.
149. Child marriages were always contracts de futuro requiring consent of the parties upon reaching the legal age, fourteen for the boy and twelve for the girl.
150. Alleman, pp. 125-126.
151. Ibid., p. 125.
152. Ibid., p. 135.
153. Quoted in Powell, pp. 149-150.
154. The issue is by no means settled. Special councils of the Presbyterian Church in the United States in 1962-63 sessions reexamined women's nature on Scriptural basis as a preliminary step to determine their fitness for increased participation in church government and the ministry.
155. Quoted in Powell, p. 147.
156. Jonathan Swift, "Of the Education of Ladies," The Prose Works of Jonathan Swift, ed. Herbert Davis (Oxford, 1957), IV, 228.
157. H.J.C. Grierson, "Love Poetry," Cross Currents in English Literature of the Seventeenth Century (London, 1929), p. 134.
158. Powell, p. 171.
159. Grierson, p. 160.
160. Powell, 160.
161. Daniel Defoe, An Essay on Projects, reprinted in William P. Trent, Daniel Defoe, How To Know Him (Indianapolis, 1916), p. 15.
162. Ibid., pp. 20-21.
163. Louis B. Wright, Middle-Class Culture in Elizabethan England (Chapel Hill, 1935), p. 103.

164. Wright, pp. 104-105.
165. Ibid., pp. 11, 114.
166. Myra Reynolds in The Learned Lady in England, 1650-1760, (New York, 1920), pp. 372-400, traces the satiric representations of the learned lady in comedy.
167. Jonathan Swift, "A Letter to a Very Young Lady on Her Marriage," Prose Works, IX, 89, 92.
168. Reynolds, p. 343.
169. George Savile, Marquis of Halifax, "Advice to a Daughter," The Complete Works, ed. Walter Raleigh (Oxford, 1912), pp. 7-19.
170. Cited in the unpub. disser. of Florence M. Hoagland, "The Women of Addison and Steele: Their Status in the Early Eighteenth Century" (Cornell, 1933), p. 101.

BIBLIOGRAPHY

Alleman, Gellert Spencer. Matrimonial Law and the Materials of Restoration Comedy. Wallingford, Pa.: The author, 1942.

Allen, Walter. The English Novel. New York: E. P. Dutton, 1954.

Alter, Robert. Fielding and the Nature of the Novel. Cambridge, Mass.: Harvard University Press, 1968.

Ashley, Maurice. England in the Seventeenth Century. Baltimore: Penguin Books, 1958.

Baker, Ernest A. The History of the English Novel. 10 vols. London: H. F. & G. Witherby, 1929-39.

Banerji, H.K. Henry Fielding, Playwright, Journalist, and Master of the Art of Fiction. Oxford: Basil Blackwell, 1929.

Battestin, Martin C. "Fielding's Changing Politics and Joseph Andrews." PQ, XXXIX (1960), 39-55.

———. The Moral Basis of Fielding's Art: A Study of Joseph Andrews. Middletown, Conn.: Wesleyan University Press, 1959.

———. "Fielding's Definition of Wisdom: Some Functions of Ambiguity and Emblem in Tom Jones." ELH, XXXV, 188-217.

Baugh, Albert C., and others. A Literary History of England. New York: Appleton-Century-Crofts, 1948.

Bayne-Powell, Rosamond. Eighteenth-Century London Life. London: John Murray, 1937.

Bell, Michael D. "Pamela's Wedding and the Marriage of the Lamb," PQ, XLIX (1970), 100-112.

Berlin, Isaiah, ed. The Age of Enlightenment. Boston: Houghton Mifflin, 1956.

Bernbaum, Ernest. The Drama of Sensibility. Gloucester, Massachusetts: P. Smith, 1958.

Birdsall, Virginia Ogden. Wild Civility: The English Comic Spirit on the Restoration Stage. Indiana University Press, 1970.

Bissell, Frederick O. Fielding's Theory of the Novel. Ithaca: Cornell University Press, 1933.

Blanchard, Frederic T. Fielding the Novelist. New Haven: Yale University Press, 1927.

Blanchard, Rae. "Richard Steele and the Status of Women." SP, XXVI (1929), 325-355.

Boas, Richard P., and Barbara M. Hahn. Social Backgrounds of English Literature. Boston: Little, Brown, 1923.

Bradley, Rose M. The English Housewife in the Seventeenth and Eighteenth Centuries. London: Edward Arnold, 1912.

Bullitt, John M. Jonathan Swift and the Anatomy of Satire. Cambridge: Harvard University Press, 1953.

Butt, John. Fielding. Writers and Their Work Series, no. 57. London: Longmans, Green, 1954.

Cecil, Lord David. Jane Austen. Cambridge: At the University Press, 1935.

Coley, William B. "The Background of Fielding's Laughter." ELH XXVI (1959).

Coolidge, J.S. "Fielding and Conservation of Character." MP, LVIII (1960), 245-259.

Cross, Wilbur L. The History of Henry Fielding. 3 vols. New Haven: Yale University Press, 1918.

Digéon, Aurelien. The Novels of Fielding. London: George Routledge & Sons, 1925.

——. Le Texte des Romans de Fielding. Paris: Hachette, 1923.

Dobrée, Bonamy. Restoration Comedy. Oxford: At the Clarendon Press, 1924.

Dobson, Austin. Fielding. New York: Harper & Brothers, 1883.

Donaldson, Ian. The World Upside-Down: Comedy from Johnson to Fielding. Oxford: At the Clarendon Press, 1970.

Dudden, F. Homes. Henry Fielding, His Life, Works, and Times. 2 vols. Oxford: At the Clarendon Press, 1952.

Dussinger, John A. "What Pamela Knew: An Interpretation," JEGP, LX (1970), 377-393.

Empson, William. "Tom Jones." Kenyon Review, XX (1958), 217-249.

Epton, Nina. Love and the English. New York: Collier Books, 1960.

Ewald, William B. , Jr. The Masks of Jonathan Swift. Cambridge: Harvard University Press, 1954.

"Fielding." London Times Literary Supplement, LIII (October 8, 1954), 641.

Fielding, Henry. Amelia. Introd. George Saintsbury, New York: E.P. Dutton, 1930.

———. The Covent-Garden Journal. Ed. Gerard E. Jensen. 2 vols. New Haven: Yale University Press, 1915.

———. Jonathan Wild and The Journal of a Voyage to Lisbon. Introd. George Saintsbury. New York: E.P. Dutton, 1932.

———. Joseph Andrews and Shamela. Ed. Martin C. Battestin. Boston: Houghton Mifflin, 1961.

———. Joseph Andrews. Introd. Maynard Mack. New York: Rinehart, 1952.

———. Shamela. Introd. Ian Watt. Augustan Reprint Society, No. 57. Los Angeles: University of California Press, 1956.

———. Tom Jones. Introd. George Saintsbury. New York. E.P. Dutton, 1947.

——. The Works of Henry Fielding. Ed. Leslie Stephen. 10 vols. London: Smith, Elder, 1882.

——. Works. With "An Essay on his Life and Genius" by Arthur Murphy. Ed. Sir Walter Scott. New York: Leavitt and Allen, [18?].

Forster, E. M. Aspects of the Novel. New York: Harcourt Brace & World, 1954.

Frye, Northrop. Anatomy of Criticism: Four Essays. Princeton: Princeton University Press, 1957.

Fujimura, Thomas H. The Restoration Comedy of Wit. Princeton: Princeton University Press, 1952.

Gagen, Jean Elisabeth. The New Woman: Her Emergence in English Drama, 1600-1730. New York: Twayne, 1954.

Godden, Gertrude M. Henry Fielding. London: Sampson Low, Marton, 1910.

Goldberg, Homer. The Art of Joseph Andrews. Chicago: University of Chicago Press, 1969.

Golder, Morris. Fielding's Moral Psychology. Amherst, 1966.

Grierson, Herbert J. C. Cross Currents in English Literature of the Seventeenth Century. London: Chatto & Windus, 1929.

Habakkuk, H. J. "Marriage Settlements in the Eighteenth Century." Transactions of the Royal Historical Society, Fourth Series, XXXII, 15-30.

Hatfield, Glenn W. "The Serpent and the Dove: Fielding's Irony and the Prudence Theme of Tom Jones." MP, LXV (1967), 17-32.

——. Henry Fielding and the Language of Irony. Chicago: University of Chicago Press, 1968.

Hoagland, Florence M. "The Women of Addison and Steele: Their Status in Early Eighteenth Century." Ms. Ph.D. Diss., Cornell University, 1933.

Hopkins, Bessie C. "The Concept of the Ruling Passion as Treated in Certain Works of Alexander Pope and Henry Fielding." Ms Master's Thesis, University of Alabama, 1948.

Howard, George E. A History of Matrimonial Institutions. 3 vols. Chicago: University of Chicago Press, 1904.

Hutchens, Eleanor N. "'Prudence' in Tom Jones: A Study of Connotative Irony." PQ, XXXIX (1960), 496-507.

Irwin, William Robert. The Making of Jonathan Wild. New York: Columbia University Press, 1941.

———. "Satire and Comedy in the Works of Henry Fielding." ELH, XIII (1946), 168-188.

Jeaffreson, John Cordy. Brides and Bridals. 2 vols. London: Hurst and Blackett, 1872.

Jenkins, Elizabeth. Henry Fielding. London: Home and Van Thal 1947.

Jensen, Gerard E. "Fashionable Society in Fielding's Time." PMLA, XXXI (1916), 78-89.

Johnson, Maurice. "The Device of Sophia's Muff in Tom Jones." MLN, LXXIV (1959), 685-690.

———. Fielding's Art of Fiction. Philadelphia: University of Pennsylvania Press, 1961.

Jones, Benjamin M. Henry Fielding, Novelist and Magistrate. London: George Allen & Unwin, 1933.

Kettle, Arnold. An Introduction to the English Novel. 2 vols. London: Hutchinson's University Library, 1951.

Kreissman, Bernard. Pamela-Shamela. University of Nebraska Studies, n.x. No. 22. Lincoln: University of Nebraska Press, 1960.

Kronenberger, Louis. Kings and Desperate Men, Life in Eighteenth-Century England. New York: Alfred A. Knopf, 1942.

Krutch, Joseph Wood. Comedy and Conscience after the Restoration.
New York: Columbia University Press, 1948.

Lawrence, Frederic, The Life of Henry Fielding. London: A.
Hall, Virtue, 1855.

Leavis, F.R. The Great Tradition. New York: G.W. Stewart,
1948.

Lewis, C.S. "Donne and Love Poetry in the Seventeenth Century."
Seventeenth Century Studies Presented to Sir Herbert
Grierson. Introd. Dover Wilson. Oxford: At the Clarendon
Press, 1938.

Loftis, John. Comedy and Society from Congreve to Fielding.
Stanford: Stanford University Press, 1959.

Lynch, Kathleen M. The Social Mode of Restoration Comedy.
New York: Macmillan, 1926.

McCutcheon, Roger P. "Amelia, or the Distressed Wife." MLN,
XLII (1927), 32-33.

McKillop, Alan D. The Early Masters of English Fiction.
Lawrence: University of Kansas Press, 1956.

——. "Personal Relations between Fielding and Richardson."
MP, XXVIII (1931), 432-433.

——. Samuel Richardson, Printer and Novelist. Chapel Hill:
University of North Carolina Press, 1936.

——. "Some Recent Views of Tom Jones." College English,
XXI (1959), 17-22.

Mandeville, Bernard. The Fable of the Bees. Ed. F.B. Kaye.
2 vols. Oxford: At the Clarendon Press, 1924.

Mason, John E. Gentlefolk in the Making, Studies in the History
of English Courtesy Literature and Related Topics from 1531
to 1774. Philadelphia: University of Pennsylvania Press,
1935.

Moore, R.E. "Dr. Johnson on Fielding and Richardson." PMLA,
LXVI (1951), 162-181.

Muir, Kenneth. The Comedy of Manners. London: Hutchinson University Library; 1970.

Murry, John Middleton. Unprofessional Essays. London: Jonathan Cape, 1956.

Nettleton, George Henry. English Drama of the Restoration and Eighteenth Century (1642-1780). New York: Macmillan, 1914.

Nicoll, Allardyce. A History of Early Eighteenth Century Drama, 1700-1750. Cambridge: At the University Press, 1925.

Noyes, Gertrude E. Bibliography of Courtesy and Conduct Books in Seventeenth-Century England. New Haven: Tuttle, Morehouse and Taylor, 1937.

Palmer, John. The Comedy of Manners. London: G. Bell & Sons, 1913.

Park, William. "Fielding and Richardson." PMLA, LXXXI, 381-388.

Perry, Henry Ten Eyck. The Comic Spirit in Restoration Drama. New Haven: Yale University Press, 1925.

Plumb, John H. The First Four Georges. London: B. T. Batsford, 1956.

Pollock, Sir Frederick, and Frederic W. Maitland. The History of English Law before the Time of Edward I. 2nd ed. 2 vols. Cambridge: At the University Press, 1911.

Powell, Chilton Latham. English Domestic Relations, 1487-1653. New York: Columbia University Press, 1917.

Powers, Lyall H. "The Influence of the Aeneid on Fielding's Amelia." MLN, LXXI (1956), 330-336.

Pringle, Patrick. Hue and Cry: The Story of Henry and John Fielding and Their Bow Street Runners. New York: William Morrow, 1955.

Rader, Ralph W. "Ralph Cudworth and Fielding's Amelia." MLN, LXI (1956), 336-338.

Rawson, C.J. "Nature's Dance of Death." Eighteenth Century
     Studies, Two Parts: Spring, 1970, #3, III, 307-338; Summer,
     1970, #4, IV, 491-522.

———. "Some Remarks on Eighteenth-Century 'Delicacy,' with a
     Note on Hugh Kelley's False Delicacy (1768)." JEGP, LXI
     (1962), 1-13.

Reynolds, Myra. The Learned Lady, 1650-1750. Boston: Houghton
     Mifflin, 1920.

Richardson, Samuel. Clarissa. Ed. J.A. Burrell. New York:
     Random House, 1950.

———. Familiar Letters on Important Occasions. Introd. Brian
     W. Downs. New York: Dodd, Mead, 1928.

———. Pamela. Ed. William M. Sale, Jr. New York: W.W.
     Norton, 1958.

Sale, William M., Jr. "From Pamela to Clarissa." The Age of
     Johnson. Essays Presented to Chauncey Brewster Tinker.
     Ed. F.W. Hilles. New Haven: Yale University Press, 1949.

Savile, George, Marquis of Halifax. Advice to a Daughter. The
     Complete Works. Ed. Walter Raleigh. Oxford: At the
     Clarendon Press, 1912.

Selley, Walter Thomas. England in the Eighteenth Century.
     A. & C. Black, 1949.

Shapiro, Charles, ed. Twelve Original Essays on Great English
     Novels. Detroit: Wayne State University Press, 1960.

Sherbo, Arthur. English Sentimental Drama. East Lansing:
     Michigan State University Press, 1957.

———. Studies in the Eighteenth Century Novel. Michigan State
     University Press, 1969.

Sherburn, George. "Fielding's Amelia: An Interpretation." ELH,
     III (1936), 1-14.

———. "Fielding's Social Outlook." PQ, XXXV (1956), 1-23.

Sherwood, Irma Z. "The Novelists as Commentators." The Age of Johnson. Essays Presented to Chauncey Brewster Tinker. Ed. F.W. Hilles. New Haven: Yale University Press, 1949.

Shesgreen, Sean. "The Moral Function of Thwackum, Square, and Allworthy." Studies in the Novel, 2 (1970), 159-167.

Smith, John Harrington. The Gay Couple. Cambridge: Harvard University Press, 1948.

Smith, J. Oates. "Masquarade and Marriage." BSUF, VI, iii (1965), 10-21.

Stephen, Leslie. English Literature and Society in the Eighteenth Century. London: Duckworth, 1927.

——. History of English Thought in the Eighteenth Century. 2 vols. New York: G.P. Putnam's Sons, 1927.

Stephens, John C., Jr. "Verge of Court and Arrest for Debt in Fielding's Amelia." MLN, LXIII (1948), 104-109.

Stevenson, Lionel. The English Novel: A Panorama. Boston: Houghton Mifflin, 1960.

Sutherland, James R. English Satire. Cambridge: At the University Press, 1958.

Swift, Jonathan. The Prose Works of Jonathan Swift. Ed. Herbert Davis. 13 vols. Oxford: Basil Blackwell, 1941-1959.

Taylor, Dick, Jr. "Joseph as Hero of Joseph Andrews." Tulane Studies, VII (1957), 91-109.

Thomas, D.S. "Fortune and the Passions in Amelia." MLR, LX (1965), 176-187.

Thompson, Charles J.S. Love, Marriage, and Romance in Old London. London: Heath, Cranton, 1936.

Thornbury, Ethel M. Henry Fielding's Theory of the Comic Prose Epic. University of Wisconsin Studies in Language and Literature No. 30. Madison: University of Wisconsin Press, 1931.

Towers, Augustus R. "Amelia and the State of Matrimony." Review of English Studies, n. s. V (1954), 144-157.

——. "Fielding and Dr. Samuel Clark." MLN, LXX (1955), 257-260.

——. "An Introduction and Annotations for a Critical Edition of Amelia." Ms. Ph. D. Diss., Princeton, 1952.

Traill, Henry D., and J.S. Mann. Social England. 6 vols. in 2. New York: G. P. Putnam's Sons, 1909.

Trent, William P. Daniel Defoe, How to Know Him. Indianapolis: Bobbs-Merrill, 1916.

Trevelyan, George M. England Under Queen Anne. 3 vols. London: Longmans, Green, 1930-34.

——. Illustrated English Social History. 4 vols. London: Longmans, Green, 1949-1952.

Turberville, Arthus S. English Men and Manners in the Eighteenth Century. New York: Oxford University Press, 1957.

Utter, Robert P., and Gwendolyn Needham. Pamela's Daughters. New York: Macmillan, 1937.

Van Ghent, Dorothy. The English Novel, Form and Function. New York: Rinehart, 1953.

Vernon, P. F. "Marriage of Convenience and the Moral Code of Restoration Comedy." Essays in Criticism, XII (1962), 370-387.

Wagnknecht, Edward. Cavalcade of the English Novel. New York Henry Holt, 1954.

Wagner, Anthony R. English Ancestry. London: Oxford University Press, 1961.

Watt, Ian P. The Rise of the Novel: Studies in Defoe, Richardson, and Fielding. Berkeley: University of California Press, 1957.

Weinkrot, Howard. "Chastity and Interpolation: Two Aspects of Joseph Andrews." JEGP, LXIX, 14-31.

Wendt, Alan. "The Naked Virtue of Amelia." ELH, XXVII, (1960),
    137-148.

Willcoeks, Mary P. A True-Born Englishman. London: Allen &
    Unwin, 1947.

Willey, Basil. The Eighteenth Century Background. New York:
    Columbia University Press, 1941.

Wolff, Cynthia G. "Fielding's Amelia: Private Virtue and Public
    Good." TSLL, X (1968), 37-55.

Woods, Charles B. "Miss Lucy Plays of Fielding and Garrick."
    PQ, XLI (1962), 294-310.

———. "Notes on Three of Fielding's Plays." PMLA, LII (1937),
    359-373.

Work, James A. "Henry Fielding, Christian Censor." The Age of
    Johnson. Essays Presented to Chauncey Brewster Tinker.
    Ed. F.W. Hilles. New Haven: Yale University Press, 1949.

Wright, Andrew H. Henry Fielding: Mask and Feast. Berkeley:
    University of California Press, 1965.

———. Jane Austen's Novels, A Study in Structure. New York:
    Oxford University Press, 1953.

Wright, Louis B. Middle-Class Culture in Elizabethan England.
    Chapel Hill: University of North Carolina Press, 1935.

Wright, Walter F. Sensibility in English Prose Fiction, 1760-1814.
    Urbana: University of Illinois Press, 1937.

Zinn, Zea. "Love and Marriage in the Novels of English Women
    (1740-1840)." Ms. Ph.D. Diss., University of Wisconsin,
    1935.

Booth, Billy, criticism of, 98, 107-111; evolution of Christian be-
    lief of, 98, 109, 111-116; as victim of social environment, 101,
    109-111; as man of feeling, 104; as center of action of novel,
    107-116; compared with Tom Jones, 108-109; as ideal husband,
    109; shortcomings of, 109-110; compared to other male char-
    acters of Amelia, 110-111, 114; debate of, with deist-fatalist
    Robinson, 111-112; involvement of, with Miss Matthews, 113-
    114; debate of, with Stoic, 114
Celibacy, glorified by church, 124
"Cits," 28, 34
Chastity, equated with virtue, 47; Joseph as male exemplar of,
    51-57; Tom's lack of, 77-81
Clandestine marriage. See Marriage, legal aspects.
Clarissa, 84, 85
Courtship, conventions of fashionable, 28-30; of sentimentalized
    lovers, 31-34; idealized, in Fielding, 32-34; of Fanny and
    Joseph, 57; of Jonathan and Laetitia (Jonathan Wild), 63-64; of
    Sophia and Tom, 88; of Amelia and Booth, 99-101.
Covent-Garden Journal, trial of Amelia in, 67, 96
Daniel, Mary. See Fielding, Mary Daniel.
Defoe, Daniel, on "cits," 34; picaresque heroines of, 43-44; on
    the matrimonial market, 45-46; on education of women, 138-
    139
Digressive stories: In Joseph Andrews, 60-61; in Jonathan Wild,
    67-69
Divorce, 130-133; by Parliamentary decree, 130, 132; separation
    by mutual consent as form of, 130-131; ecclesiastical forms of,
    130; impediments as basis for annulment, 131-132; jactitation
    of marriage, 132-133
Eighteenth-century comedy. See Restoration comedy; see also
    Sentimental comedy.
Fathers, The, 31; 35
Fielding, Charlotte Cradock, Fielding's courtship of, 12-16; por-
    trait of, as Sophia, 14-15; portrait of, as Amelia, 15; Field-
    ing's marriage to, 15-18; death of, 18
Fielding, Edmund, 9
Fielding, Mary Daniel, Fielding's marriage to, 18-21
Fielding, Henry (See also specific topic headings and individual
    titles.), family quarrels experienced in boyhood, 9; attempted
    abduction of Sarah Andrews by, 9-11; as dramatist, 11, 16, 23-
    42; courtship of and marriage to Charlotte Cradock, 12-18; role